Consequences
A Unique Approach to Financial
Planning for Young Adults

John Blankenship

First Edition
April 2008

The information in this book is intended for educational use only. Some concepts have been intentionally simplified to make them easier to understand. The goal is to make young adults aware that they have many choices in life, and that they will be better prepared to achieve the things they want if they can evaluate the long-range consequences of the decisions they have to make.

John Blankenship

Contents

Preface

The decisions you make when you are young can dramatically change your life. Unfortunately, most people don't know their options, let alone the consequences of acting on those options. Properly saving just $6 each month, for example, can increase your retirement wealth by nearly $70,000. Just changing the way you buy your cars can add a MILLION dollars to your retirement nest egg.

Life offers many choices. Unfortunately, we often make those choices without knowing the long-range consequences of our decisions. You can't make intelligent decisions if you don't understand how each of your choices will affect your life. The purpose of this book is to give you the information and skills needed to better predict the future value of the choices you face.

Early chapters will show how simple decisions, made while you are young, can make huge changes in your financial future. Once this knowledge has motivated you to learn more, subsequent chapters will explore the principles of saving and investing, including such topics as boosting your returns, decreasing your risks, and minimizing your taxes, but none of these subjects will be examined in the usual way.

Most books tell you *what you should do* – this book does not. Instead, you will learn about financial planning by exploring the consequences associated with various choices. After you understand the basic principles, you will learn how to use a computer program to help evaluate your options. As you learn to predict the ramifications of your decisions, you will be able to make the choices that are best for you.

Making the right choices in life helps you obtain the financial future you desire. Wealth does not come without sacrifice, but unless you know how much benefit you can receive from various sacrifices, you can't determine which ones are right for you. Understanding your choices and their consequences puts you in charge of your life. Not understanding them leaves your financial future to chance.

The choice is yours!

Chapter 1
Choices and Consequences

Since you're reading this book it is likely that you fall into the young adult category and that means you, as well as other young adults, probably spend very little time thinking about your financial future. Unfortunately, right now, while you have a long life ahead of you, is precisely the time when you *should* be considering your financial alternatives. As you will soon see, the decisions you make today can have an enormous impact on your future.

This book is very different from other books that offer financial advice because it does not try to tell you what you *should* do. I don't know you (or your dreams or goals) so there is no way I can decide what is best for you. I can, however, help you understand that there are many options available to you, even though you are probably unaware of many of them. I will also help you see that the choices you make, as you confront your options, will have long-range consequences. Understanding, not only the consequences themselves, but *how* your decisions bring about those consequences can give you the ability to make better choices – choices that can help you obtain what *you* really want from life.

No matter how simple or obvious this idea seems though, the unfortunate truth is that it is not unusual for people to make decisions early in life that greatly reduce their chances of reaching their desired goals. Relatives and friends see young adults making some of the mistakes they themselves made, and they want to prevent those they care about from following in their footsteps. In your own life, you may have noticed that well-meaning friends and relatives seem to have an endless supply of advice as to how you should lead your life. The problem of course, is that their ideas, no matter how fantastic they are, may be perfect for them, but are not necessarily right for you.

The good news is that because you are young, even minor changes in your behavior today can often cause massive changes in the future. The bad news is that the younger you are, the further away the future seems, and the further it seems, the less it matters to you. Let's clarify this concept by examining it in very specific terms. Using specific terms means that we must use numbers and that requires a little mathematics. Don't despair though, nothing we have to do is hard to understand. Besides, once you understand the principles we will develop, you'll find that you seldom have to be concerned with any of the mathematical details. Stick with me. I *promise*, by the end of Chapter 3 you will be excited.

Enough of this though, let's jump right into an example. Suppose that I told you, assuming that you are around age 20, that giving up a fast-food lunch just once each month (don't focus too much on skipping lunch; this is just an example to demonstrate a point) could result in you having an extra $70,000 when you retire in your mid 60's. Your first reaction would probably be that you don't believe it, and that is a very key point. If you don't believe something, then you won't even consider it as a potential option when you analyze your alternatives. The $70,000 figure, by the way, is a realistic estimate and I will prove it to you later in this chapter. First, though, I want to revisit the idea that I'm not here to tell you what choices are right for you.

Some people will choose *not* to give up one lunch each month even if they know that it will give them an additional $70,000 when they retire. Others may get really excited about the prospect and decide to give up two lunches each month in order to have an extra $140,000. Only you can decide what is best for you. If you are unaware of the consequences associated with giving up one or more lunches though, you effectively eliminate your option of making *any* of these choices.

Giving up one lunch each month may seem like a minor thing, but remember, in order to get the $70,000 you have to give up one lunch every month for about forty-five years. That is a big sacrifice for many people and unless they are convinced that the sacrifice will result in an acceptable payoff, it is unlikely that they will continue making the sacrifice over the years.

You have many more options available to you though. For example, what if you only give up one lunch each month for the next five years instead of your whole life. How do you think this would compare to the forty-five year choice? The answer may surprise you. Even though you sacrifice for only five years instead of forty-five, you will still create more than $27,000 of retirement funds, nearly half as much reward for a small fraction of the sacrifice.

The timing of decisions can very important. Again, let's look at a specific example to help clarify the concept. In the above alternative, giving up one lunch a month for five years gave you $27,000. How do you think that would change if, instead of giving up the lunches over the *next* five years, you gave up lunches during the five years immediately preceding your retirement? The later choice will net you less than $500. This is a valuable piece of information. Notice that the rewards for the two situations were dramatically different even though you essentially made the same sacrifice (one lunch each month for five years).

It is also important to realize that these are only some of many choices available to you. For example, if you think five years is too long, you could consider giving up a lunch each month for only one year or perhaps if you are only going to sacrifice for one year, you might consider giving up one lunch every week. Without knowing the value of these sacrifices though, you cannot possibly decide which is best or even if either of them is worth considering. I hope you are wondering what each of these new options are worth. Giving up one lunch each month for one year nets you a measly $6,600 at retirement, but giving up one each week for one year is even more lucrative ($28,600) than giving up one every week for five years ($27,000).

Hopefully you are starting to get the idea. Life is full of choices we often don't even consider, and even if we did, we would probably do a poor job of evaluating the long-range consequences associated with making those choices. All choices have both costs and benefits. Only you can decide what choices are right for you. The important point here is that you can't make intelligent choices if you don't understand the long-range consequences of your options. The goal of this book is to help you learn how to estimate the value of the choices you are considering so that you can decide if they are right for you.

All of the examples in this chapter assume your lunch costs $6, so it is easy to make substitutions. Any sacrifice that results in a savings of $6 will have the same effect. For example, bringing a packed lunch from home twice might result in the same overall savings as totally skipping one visit to McDonald's. Or, you could consider other options such as choosing a small popcorn at the movies instead of a large. It doesn't even have to be a monthly thing. Buying one less video game (at $72) every year has the same effect as saving $6 every month.

As you can see, you really do have many choices in your life – choices that can dramatically alter your financial future. In order to make them intelligently, you must know how to appraise the long-range value of your decisions. Understanding how your decisions can actually create wealth is vital. If you don't truly understand, then you won't believe, and if you don't believe you won't have the will power to stick with the decisions you make. And now, just as I promised, it is time to show you exactly how a savings of $6 a month can turn into $70,000 at retirement.

First, let's summarize the facts. We will assume that you are going to add $6 every month (starting at age 20) to some form of saving or investment account. We will also assume that the account will generate an average return of 10%. Later chapters will show how to achieve this return over your life with minimal risk.

Figure 1.1 shows the amount of money accumulated in the account after each year. Let's look at a few examples to make sure everything is clear. The first year you save $6 for 12 months giving a total saved of $72. If we add the accumulated interest of $3 (see the next paragraph for details), the total after the first year becomes $75.

If you have been following the calculations carefully, you might have expected to have a $7.20 return (10% of $72) at the end of the first year. This would only be true if you had the entire $72 invested for the entire year, which is not that case. At the end of the first month, for example, only $6 was earning a return for you. The actual return earned during the first year is about $3.39, which is rounded in the table to the closest dollar.

At the end of the second year you will have the $75 you started with, the $72 you contributed during the second year, and an earned return of $12 for a total of $159. These may seem like small sums when compared to the sacrifice of giving up a lunch every month, but watch what happens as the years go by. By age 40 (20 years) your account is worth over $5,000 and by age 60 (another 20 years) it is nearly $42,000. Notice that the first 20 years generated

5

only $5000 while the second 20 years added nearly $37,000. How could this be? After all, you saved exactly the same amount of money during both 20-year periods (20 years * $72/year = $1440). Just as in a previous example, timing is an important factor.

Age	Total $ Accumulated	Age	Total $ Accumulated
20	75	43	7138
21	159	44	7961
22	251	45	8870
23	352	46	9874
24	465	47	10984
25	589	48	12209
26	726	49	13563
27	877	50	15059
28	1044	51	16711
29	1229	52	18536
30	1433	53	20552
31	1659	54	22780
32	1908	55	25241
33	2183	56	27959
34	2487	57	30962
35	2823	58	34280
36	3194	59	37944
37	3603	60	41993
38	4056	61	46466
39	4556	62	51407
40	5109	63	56865
41	5719	64	62895
42	6393	65	69556

Figure 1.1: Saving only $6 a month can create nearly $70,000 by retirement.

The reason timing is important is because of a concept called *compounding*. We will discuss compounding in detail in later chapters, but let's examine it briefly here. While it is true, that you are only contributing $6 every month to your accumulating wealth, the amount of money being contributed *by the wealth itself* is slowly growing. This simply means the more money you have, the more it contributes. Let's look at an example.

Remember, during the first year (age 20), the 10% return added only $3 to your account. This meant that the total new money added was $75 (your contribution of $72 plus the $3 return – money essentially contributed by your accumulated wealth). During the second year, the return was $12 (substantially higher than the first year amount of $3) because you had more money in your account. At age 40 you are still contributing $72 each year, just as before. Since you have accumulated more than $5000 by then though, the 10% return from your accumulated wealth generates around $500 every year. By age 60, the earnings from your wealth are contributing over $4000 every year even if you don't contribute a penny yourself. This is a very powerful idea that deserves further examination.

Remember, at the beginning of this chapter it was stated that you could accumulate $27,000 if you saved for only five years. Now you can see how this is possible. At the end of five years you will have accumulated almost $500. This means that your wealth would contribute nearly $50 (assuming a 10% return) even if you stopped your contribution of $72. And don't forget, as your wealth increases over time, the amount it contributes will also increase.

Understanding the above principle should help you realize the importance of being able to evaluate the value of the options available to you. Suppose, for example, you have decided you want to start skipping one lunch each month, but you are considering waiting a few years before you start the process. Wouldn't it be nice to know the consequence of waiting? How valuable would it be if you could quickly examine many different choices and compare the long-range ramifications of those choices? Later chapters will give you that opportunity by providing a computer program that will let you play *what-if* with nearly any option you can imagine.

The whole purpose of this chapter was to get your attention – to help you realize that even the *small* choices you make can have dramatic consequences for your future. Chapter 2 will become even more dramatic because it begins to look at more complex choices and situations.

By the time you get to the end of Chapter 3 you should be thoroughly motivated and ready for a detailed examination of financial ideas and principles. Don't think for a moment that a detailed examination has to be intimidating. Financial ideas and principles don't have to be complicated if they are explained properly. Once you recognize that you have many options available to you and understand how to evaluate the impact various options will have on your life, you will be better able to make decisions that will help you achieve your goals.

Before we continue, remember what you have learned from this chapter. For every $6 you save every month, you will have nearly $70,000 when you retire. If you don't think that sounds like a lot of money, consider how much you will have if you saved $100 a month.

Chapter 2
Bigger Choices, Bigger Rewards

Chapter 1 explored the idea that even very small changes in your behavior can lead to significant rewards. This chapter will continue the discussion by examining how extraordinary rewards can be obtained by dealing with more complex choices. One of the powerful conclusions of this chapter will be that complex choices don't always have to be as difficult to implement as you might imagine.

Before we continue, let me warn you that this chapter, like the last one, does involve some mathematics. This is the last chapter we will need this kind of detail so bear with me just a little longer. At this point in the book it really is important for you to see proof that the assertions I make are true. You don't have to understand every detail, but please, if the claims don't seem possible, study the examples until you are convinced they are true.

Nearly everyone buys a car these days and most take it for granted that when they are ready to buy, that they should go to the bank for a loan. The idea of paying cash for their cars is an unthinkable option for the vast majority of people. Before you reject the idea of paying cash for your cars though, let's examine some scenarios that could make this possible.

Normally, when a person wants a car, they borrow the money, buy the car, and then make payments for the life of the loan. What if we could reverse this process – that is, make the payments first, and then buy the car. I know this idea probably sounds ridiculous, but bear with me. The final result will be worth it.

The biggest argument against making your payments before you buy your car is that you need the car now. Of course, you could postpone the need for a car if you rode the bus or lived near your work, but those are not acceptable solutions for many people. Let's look at one solution that might be more tolerable. Assume you are just out of school and need a car immediately to get to your first job. Let's further assume that you acquire a four-year loan for $10,000 with payments of $254/month, and buy a car. (Note: If you want to buy $20,000 cars, for example, just double all the numbers throughout this illustration.) At the end of the four-year loan period, most people are tired of the car and trade it in on another (borrowing more money and continuing to make payments to the bank).

But let's assume you are not going to be like most people. When your loan is paid, you decide to drive your car for four more years. That choice already makes you different from most people, but let's also assume that you decide to continue making payments even though your car is paid for (thus making the payments *before* you buy your next car). You will make these new payments to yourself, into an investment account (like we did with the saved lunch-money in Chapter 1).

During the first four-year period you will pay the bank 48 payments of $254 for a total of $12,192. Of course, $10,000 of that sum pays the bank back the money you owe them – the other $2,192 is the interest you pay the bank to compensate them for letting you use their money for four years. Interest is a lot like rent. The interest you pay the bank is basically a rental fee for using their money.

If you pay the same payments to yourself during the next four years your account will accumulate the entire

$12,192. Your account will be even larger though, because the money in your account will have earned interest for you (the bank is now paying you for letting them use your money). If you can average a 10% return each year, you could have an additional $2,724 at the end of the second four years. This means your account will total $14,916. Figure 2.1 shows this amount as the first entry in the table.

From this point on, we will assume you buy a new car (at least a car new to you) every four years. (Note: Since you can sell or trade in your old car, you will constantly get a more expensive car.) The good news is that you don't have to go to the bank for a loan. Since you have $14,916 in your account, just remove $10,000 and pay cash for a car. This leaves $4,916 in your account.

If you had gone to the bank like most people, you would have to continue making car payments during the next four years. In your case, you too will make payments (even though you just paid cash for your car), but into your investment account just like you did in the previous four years. At the end of the next four years your account will have grown substantially.

At the end of this four-year period, you will have the $4,916 you started with, plus the $12,192 you paid in as payments during the four years. Recall that during the previous four-year period, your money earned a return for you of $2,724. During this period, you will earn a return, not only on the money you contributed, but also on the $4,916 you started with. This will result in a total earnings of $5,129, bringing the total in your account to $22,236 (4,916 + 12,192 + 5,129).

Since it has been four years since your last car, you remove $10,000 and purchase another car (for cash) leaving $12,236 in your account. During the next four years you continue to make payments to yourself just as before. Since the money in your account is growing, the money it is earning is also growing, causing the total in

11

your account to reach $33,140. If you continue this process for 11 or 12 cars (which should put you at a retirement age) your account will total somewhere around a million dollars, as shown in Figure 2.1.

Car	Fin. Cost	Cash Cost	Earnings[*]	Acc. Savings
1	$12,192	$10,000	$2,724	$14,916
2	12,192	10,000	5,129	22,236
3	12,192	10,000	8,711	33,140
4	12,192	10,000	14,047	49,379
5	12,192	10,000	21,994	73,565
6	12,192	10,000	33,829	109,586
7	12,192	10,000	51,456	163,234
8	12,192	10,000	77,709	243,136
9	12,192	10,000	116,810	362,137
10	12,192	10,000	175,043	539,373
11	12,192	10,000	261,774	803,339
12	12,192	10,000	390,947	1,186,478
Total	$146,304	$120,000	$1,160,174	$1,186,478

([*] Earnings are rounded and may not sum exactly)

Figure 2.1: The accumulated savings from paying cash for your cars can be dramatic.

The million-dollar total might impress you, but that is not the most impressive aspect of this example. The most impressing aspect is how *similar* the overall lifetime activities are for the two choices. In the beginning you had to drive the first car for eight years or ride the bus or whatever was necessary to let you make payments for four years *before* you bought your next car. Once that initial period is over though, the activity forthcoming from both choices is *identical*. In both cases, a $10,000 car is purchased every four years. In one case, you borrow the money to buy the car and in the other you withdraw the money from your account, but in both cases you buy a new car. In both cases, payments of $254 are made every month. In one case, you give that payment to the bank while in the other you add that amount to your investment account.

Now that the similarities are apparent, let's look more closely at the differences. If you had chosen not to finance your cars, the only difference in your life would have been that initial four years where you either rode public transportation or continued to drive a previously owned car. But, in order to pay cash for your cars over your lifetime, this is the penalty you must pay. The question is, are the consequences of such a sacrifice worth it to you?

Only you can make that decision, but think about it this way. If someone came up to you today and told you they would give you a million dollars if you change *just* four years of your life. Assume they explained to you that you had to start making car payments right away, but you had to use public transportation or continue driving your old car for the next four years. Assume they also assured you that, after that four-year period, the rest of your life would not change. Either way, you would buy a new car every four years and make payments to the bank or yourself. Then they offered you a postdated check for a million dollars. Would *you* take it?

This is a choice every person is faced with. They can get instant gratification by using a loan to start driving that car immediately or they can postpone the purchase until they can pay cash. As you would expect, nearly everyone chooses to go to the bank. I believe many do so, because they don't understand the consequences of their actions. Without question, they don't understand that their decision could be costing them a million dollars later in life, but that is only part of the picture. There is another reason people choose not to pay cash for their cars. Not only do they *under*estimate the advantages of paying cash, they *over*estimate the things they must give up.

If you suggest to someone that they start paying cash for all their cars, they will usually assume that such a decision will require sacrifices over their *entire* lifetime. They will assume that either they will not be able to afford the cars they could purchase if they use loans or that they will constantly have to postpone purchases until they save enough cash. As we have seen, both of these assumptions are false. The *only* difference in the lives of the two people making these decisions is four years. When you compare the actual cost of making this decision (four years of public transportation or 4 years driving your old car) to the potential return a million dollars, you should wonder why people make the choices they do.

I think the reason is relatively simple. People today are not used to waiting for anything. Fast food is delivered to the counter before we even get our change. Television teaches us that problems can be discovered, analyzed and solved in a thirty-minute show or at most a two-hour movie. These aspects of life not only make people expect instant gratification; they discourage people from learning to *plan* for the future. It is this inability-to-plan that prevents people from properly evaluating the consequences of their choices. Planning, after-all, is nothing more than itemizing your options and comparing them so you know which ones are best for you.

The intention of this book is to help you view choices in an entirely different manner. Your future belongs to you. People can have nearly anything they want, but not without sacrifice. After you decide what you want from life, you must decide what you are willing to give up to get it. The problem is that most people don't realize how little they have to give up to make a difference nor how much they can expect to receive from making sacrifices. We are all faced with multitudes of choices. In order to maximize what we get from life, we must be able evaluate the consequences of our actions. Now that I have set the stage for what you can expect from this book, let's return to our car example.

In our example, I have said that after 12 cars or 44 years, you *could* be more than a million dollars richer than if you had chosen the finance alternative. Notice that I said *could*. In order for you to actually achieve these astonishing results, you must *not* spend the savings you are accumulating. The money must remain fully invested over the entire period. This is not a concept you should take lightly. The reason most people never accumulate any significant wealth, is not that they don't save. It is the fact that after they save a few dollars, they always seem to find something they *must* spend it on.

In order to see the significance of the above statements, let's examine where all the money in our car example came from. After all, if you financed 12 cars, as in our example, you would have only paid a total of $146,304 (12 times $12,192). Compare that with the $120,000 you would spend if you paid cash for each of the 12 cars. This means if you financed your cars, you would have spent only $26,304 more dollars over an entire lifetime,. But that really is the secret. If you keep this relatively modest sum of money invested for 44 years, it can easily earn a million dollars. I know this statement brings many questions to your mind. Rest assured, these questions, and their answers, will be addressed in later chapters in great detail. For now though, let's study the situation a little further.

The fact that the difference in cash outlay for the two situations is only $26,304 deserves a deeper analysis. As stated earlier, most people make the choices they do in life because they don't fully understand the consequences of their actions. The $26,304 is a good example. Most people don't even stop to consider how much they are spending on finance charges over their lifetime, and even if they did, they would generally draw the wrong conclusion. If you asked most people why they finance their cars, for example, it is doubtful you get any form of insightful answer. If you are very lucky, you might actually find a person that knows that the total cost is only $26,304 (for our example) over an entire lifetime. They rationalize that driving a new car every four years is worth the extra $500 or so a year they spend on interest.

Unfortunately, as we have seen, their rationalization about financing their cars instead of paying cash is wrong in two areas. First, their assumption that they would have to give up buying new cars *throughout their entire life* is wrong. As we have seen, it is only necessary to give up the car for one four-year period. Second, they assume that they only give up $26,304. They *never* consider the returns that money could generate for them if they had invested it.

In conclusion, if you make the choice to alter what you drive for one four-year period in your life, you can make a million dollar difference in your net worth at retirement. Don't let that statement slip by without realizing how powerful it is. I must emphasis that I am not suggesting that you give up things your whole life. I want you to recognize the choices that you have available, and the true value of the decisions you can make. Having this ability is the only way you will be able to intelligently make the choices that are right for you.

As a final note, consider the fact that there are many financial situations that parallel the one described above. The use of credit cards is the first one to come to mind. Most people spend their life carrying some credit card debt. For the most part, they find a way to pay off what they owe along with a huge amount of interest. They never stop to consider that if they can pay the principle *and* the interest, then they could certainly pay cash for what they wish to buy, *if they could only get caught up* (and not have to pay interest) or if they had just never started misusing their credit to begin with.

Again, most people make the wrong assumptions. They think that if they did not use credit cards they would have to give up things they need and want for their *entire* life. In reality, if they quit buying things for just a short time – just long enough to create an appropriate cash reserve – then they could use that reserve for their purchases in exactly the same way that we paid cash for cars. And, if you consider that the interest rates on credit cards is far greater than the interest rates on car loans and couple that with the fact that many people carry credit card debt at least as large as their car loan, then you will see that the consequences of credit card debt can be even more dramatic than numbers we saw with the car example.

I hope I have your attention. In the chapters that follow you are going to learn how to evaluate the consequences of your decisions as well as how to manage your investments. Some of the alternatives offered will not be right for you, but there may be others you can embrace with passion. It's always difficult to give up things in life, but I think you will find decisions much easier to make if you fully understand the resulting consequences.

Chapter 3
Accumulating Wealth

In the previous chapter, it was stated that most people can get great financial rewards later in life by making small sacrifices when they are young. The car-example demonstrated this idea but it left out a lot of important information. For example, although it was assumed that the money that accumulated as you purchased cars was invested in some way, it neglected to discuss any details of those investments. Examples of appropriate investments could be real estate, stocks, bonds, or even your own business.

Personally investing in real estate and starting your own business (contrary to late night infomercials) take both time and money, not to mention skills and knowledge appropriate for the endeavors. So, even if you are entrepreneurly inclined, you will need a way of amassing a significant amount of start-up funds if you want to improve your chances of success. In this chapter and those that follow, we will see how stocks and bonds can aid in amassing those funds. In fact, after you fully understand the nature of stocks and bonds, you might want to make them your primary investment vehicle.

Touting on the principles explored in the first chapter, this chapter will examine investing far differently that most texts. It will look at various options and what the likely consequences are for those options. As these consequences are scrutinized, you will see why various approaches to investing can increase or decrease your risk. It will also show why appropriate risks are necessary because of their potential rewards.

Now that you know a little about where this chapter is headed, let's get back to the primary topic of investing. Let's start by stating the obvious (even though people are constantly looking for some secret way of getting around this requirement). *In order to make money investing, you have to have something to invest.* In order to accumulate your initial funds, you must spend less money than you bring home. There are several ways to do this.

One of the most obvious ways to have money available for investing is to decrease your spending. Another way is to simply make more money to begin with. This might mean going to college or, if you are already going, staying longer for an advanced degree. It might mean moon-lighting at a second job or just working overtime at your primary job. If you are really serious about investing, you should *both* increase your income and decrease your spending, *at least for some period of time.* As we saw with the car example, you must be willing to sacrifice, but the sacrifices don't have to last nearly as long as most people think. This will be discussed in great detail shortly.

In order to make this concept clearer, let's examine a specific situation. Assume for a moment that you have a good job and that you can pay your bills, but have very little left over, perhaps only $100 a month. Most people would not feel that such a small sum could be the basis for a successful investment program. As we will see later, there are easy ways to invest $100 a month. But for now, let's examine the consequences of such an investment.

The graph in Figure 3.1 shows the value of your investment account over time. It assumes that you save only $100 each month starting at age 20. It assumes that you can average 10% return on your investments. This may sound like a lot, but as we will see later, this is not unreasonable at all, if you invest properly.

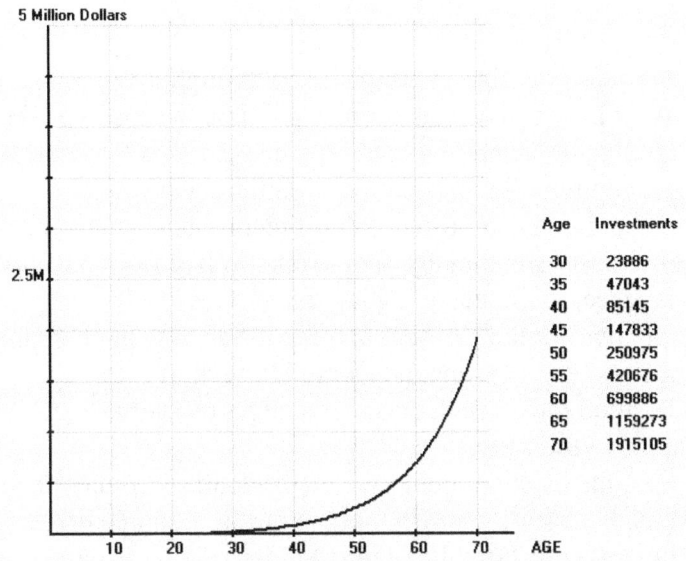

Figure 3.1: Investing only $100 a month can really mount up over time.

As you can see from Figure 3.1, even such a small monthly sum can build to a huge nest egg. By the time you are at a normal retirement age, you can easily have a million dollars or more. If you invest $200 each month, all of the amounts in the figure can be doubled. The question you need to answer is the following. *Are the sacrifices you would have to make to save $100 a month worth a million dollars?*

Before you answer that question, I want to explore your options in much more detail. Let's look very specifically at what you might have to give up to get that million dollars. You are going to see that there are many options available to you.

21

How much more could you save, if you had a better job? Over a lifetime, college graduates, for example, average three times the salary of high school graduates. If going to college allows you to save an extra $500 each month, would you think those four years were worth the $5,000,000 or more that you would have when you are ready to retire.

Perhaps you plan to go to college though, but you want to live a life of luxury as soon as possible because you feel life is a gamble and you could die in a car wreck tomorrow. Thus, you feel like you should spend every penny you make having a good time. I don't recommend such a plan, but the truth is that many people tend to live from paycheck to paycheck without saving anything. Obviously, those people live for the moment and see little value in changing their lifestyle. Perhaps they would though, if they understood the consequences of a huge, but very short change, in their life.

Assume for a moment you are graduating from college and ready to start your first job. Your new source of income would certainly be much higher than any part-time work you had in college. If you are like most people, you feel this new source of wealth deserves a new lifestyle. After all, while you were in college, you probably would have lived a fairly low-cost lifestyle. Perhaps you lived at home because your school was close by. Maybe you went away to college and lowered your housing costs by having roommates. After making these and many other sacrifices for the years of college, you might feel you deserve to live the good life.

Unfortunately, most recent graduates get a nice apartment complete with new furniture (on credit, of course), acquire a new car (and car loan), and start enjoying the good life to the point that they not only don't save anything, but often pile up thousands, if not tens-of-thousands of dollars in credit card debt in just a few years.

It is easy to tell these people that they could retire rich if they only saved a few hundred dollars a month, but some people just can't stick with such a savings program. If you are one of those people, let's examine a different approach. Assume that when you graduate from college, you continue living that inexpensive college lifestyle, but only for one year. Yes, I am suggesting that you only change a single year of your life. Let's see what the consequences might be.

Try to imagine how much you could save each month if you continued to live like a student, but had the income of a college graduate. If you could continue to live at home for one year you might have no rent at all, and if you offered to pay your parents for your food, you might even be able to convince them to accept such an arrangement for a year. Even if your job was in another city or state, you could decide to find a roommate situation and cut your rental expenses at least in half, perhaps much more if several roommates are involved.

Rent and associated expenses such as utilities are not the only expenses you could try to cut. Remember this is only for a single year. Perhaps for that year you could take your lunch instead of eating out. This could easily save $5 a day or over a $100 each month. Maybe you are willing to give up Saturday night at the bar or get a cheaper cell phone – after all, you are only doing this for one year. With a little thought you can see that many expenses can be cut or eliminated if you know that the sacrifices are temporary.

Perhaps you are thinking that there is no way that you are going to continue living like a poor student. The years at college were enough of a sacrifice and now you deserve to have something better. Maybe for *one year* you would prefer to increase your income rather than cut your expenses. If your new job offers overtime pay, you might substantially increase your income with only a modest increase in work hours.

If overtime is not available at your job, you might consider a second job for *one year*. If you love to party, perhaps you could tend bar on weekends. If you love computers, music, golf, or other hobby, perhaps you can get a retail position in that industry that will allow you to get paid as well as getting discounts on what you buy. Yes, this means you have to give up some evenings and weekends *for one year*, but before you reject the idea, lets look at the consequences.

If you followed any of the above plans, or even did a little of each, how much could you save? If you could eliminate just rent and utilities, the savings could easily be $1000 a month. If you really scrimped for the year and worked a second job you might save $2000 a month or more. For the sake of example, let's assume you decided to alter your lifestyle and save just $1000 each month for a single year. The Figure 3.2 shows the consequences of that action.

Notice the similarity of Figures 3.1 and 3.2. If you save $100 a month from age 20 to age 70, you could have over 1.9 million dollars and you have nearly the same amount (at age 70) if you saved $1000 a month for only one year of your life *even if you spent every penny you earned from your job after that one year*. How is this possible? In the first case you saved $1200 a year for 50 years for a total of $60,000. In the second, you saved only a total of $12,000 (12 months at $1000 per month). In the second case, though, all of the money was saved much earlier in your life.

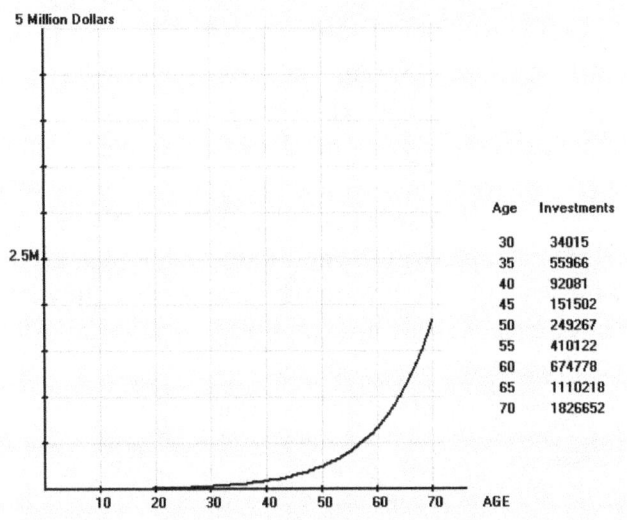

Figure 3.2: Saving $1000 each month for only one year can be rewarding.

After the first year, the income generated by the $12,000 invested at a 10% return would be $1200 each year, the exact same amount per year you would be saving if you invested $100 a month for a lifetime. This is why you can quit saving in the second example: *the money you saved that first year is making your investment contributions for you.* This powerful principle is called *compounding.* It simply means that instead of just earning money on the money *you* have saved, you also earn returns on your returns. When you invest for long periods the compound effect can be enormous and far more valuable than most people realize.

In fact, the advantage of saving early is so powerful, let's see what would happen if you waited until you were 30 to start saving $100 a month. Figure 3.3 shows the results. The total funds at age 70 have dropped by more than a million dollars. This is a huge consequence from waiting only 10 years to start your investment program. If

25

you wait until 30 to start, you would have to increase your monthly saving from $100 a month to $273 per month to end up with the same $1.9 million dollars at age 70.

The point I really want to make is that there are many ways to have the money you need. Some people might want to give up a lot for only a short period, while others might prefer a smaller sacrifice over their entire working career. Some people will see enormous value in starting early, while others will have to pay dearly when they do start to save because they are unwilling to make small sacrifices when they were younger.

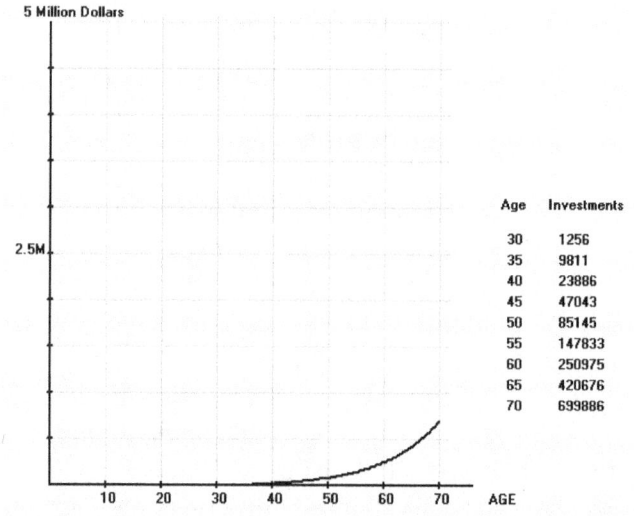

Figure 3.3: Waiting until 30 to start investing can cost you a million dollars.

In addition, I suspect many readers would like to retire much earlier than 70. Perhaps you have been wondering how much you would have to save to get the funds you want by age 50 or 60. Getting you to consider such options is really the goal of this book. Once you realize you have options, and begin to understand the consequences of those options, you can create a plan that allows you to decide what you want (financially) from life and what you are willing to give up to get it.

In order to create a plan that is right for you, though, you need an easy way of evaluating the consequences of your choices. The free companion software program for this book was used to generate the graphs used in this and several other chapters. It allows you to try different scenarios and see the long-range financial results. Another goal of this book is to make you aware of the many options available to you. After you have determined what you want financially from life, you can use the program to determine various ways of achieving your goals. Knowing the consequences for each of your choices allows you to better choose the ones that are right for you.

Everyone has to make decisions about their future, but often, especially when they are young, they don't understand the options available to them nor the consequences of those options. Many young people would choose to start investing much earlier if they understood the things revealed in this chapter. If you are already past your youth, don't despair. No matter how old your are, the best time to start investing in your future is today. The next chapter will start adding to your list of options.

Chapter 4
Stocks and Bonds

Stocks and bonds have been mentioned earlier, but now its time to delve deeper into the details associated with this form of investing. For some readers, the details described in this chapter might be both boring and overwhelming. I urge you to stick with me though, because you will need at least a modest background to really appreciate what will follow. Once you understand some basic fundamentals, I will show you how many of the details of investing can be eliminated.

Let's examine stocks first. When you own stock, you own a portion of the company. In order to raise capital to start, run, or expand a company, the founders or officers of the company might sell part of the company to others in the form of stock. In the past when you became a part-owner of a company this way, you were given a paper stock certificate showing how much owned. You can still have a certificate delivered to you when you buy stock, but today, your record of ownership is usually just a data entry in some computer.

Obviously, a major reason you would want to own stock in a company would be to make a profit. The way a company distributes profits to the stockholders is by paying *dividends*, but that is not the only way you can make money by owning stock. As an owner of a piece of a company, you have the right to sell your ownership (your stock) to someone else. If the company has expanded or grown more profitable while you owned it, then prospective buyers might be willing to purchase your stock for more than you paid for it. I say might, because there are many things that determine what people will pay for a stock. We will come back to this topic shortly.

Another way that a company can raise money when needed, is to borrow the money from someone. They perform this borrowing by issuing a *bond*. When you buy a bond, the company promises to pay you back the money they borrowed, plus a bonus for getting to use your money. This bonus is called *interest* and may referred to as the *coupon*. Generally the amount of interest to be paid is quoted as a percentage and is a fixed amount. For example, if you purchased a $1000, five-year bond with a coupon of 5%, you could expect to be paid $50 (5% of $1000) each year for five years and then you would get your $1000 back.

When you buy a bond, *theoretically*, you are taking less risk than when you buy stock. The company issuing the bond must pay you the coupon interest even if they don't make any profits. Of course, if the company does so poorly that it bankrupts, then you might never get your interest or your principle (the $1000) back. For this and other reasons we will discuss later, a corporate bond is not totally risk free, but if the issuing company is large and well run, the risk can be minimal.

Banks raise money in much the same way, and refer to the bonds they sell as *certificates-of-deposits* or CD's. The federal government issues bonds called *treasuries*. Government bonds are generally safer than corporate bonds, because the only way they can become worthless is if the government bankrupts or is overthrown. If that were to happen nearly every investment would be worthless anyway because the law of government is what insures all rights of ownership.

When you own stock in a company, you do not have the guaranteed return that you do with a bond. If the company issuing the bond has a bad year and looses money, it still has to pay its obligations to its bondholders. There is a good chance, though, that a company having a bad year will not pay any dividends. Sometimes, though, a company wants to have a reputation for paying dividends regularly. Such companies might borrow money to pay dividends when times are bad, hoping to repay the debt when times are good again.

You might be thinking that bonds are a much better investment than stocks because bonds have a guaranteed rate-of-return. In some cases (more on this later), this is definitely true, but the whole picture won't be clear till we delve a little deeper. Think about this. If a company can pay its bond debt and stay in business, then it *must* be making more profit than the interest it is paying on its outstanding bonds. If you are an owner of a company you will almost always make more money, *in the long run*, than the people that only loan money to that company. But, as we will see, the income to the owners of a company is not guaranteed. As an owner, you should expect to have great years where the profits are high and other years where you may actually loose money. Even with loses though, the *average* return for stockholders of successful companies should be larger than that of bondholders.

If we examine historical data from the thousands of companies in the United States over the past 45 years, we find that the average annual rate of return for stockholders to be around 10.5%. During that same period corporate bonds averaged a little more than 7% while government bonds returned a little less than 6% giving a bond average of about 6.5%. This means that bondholders, over time, should generally expect to earn about 4% annually less than stockholders.

The question you should be asking yourself is "Is the risk of ownership worth it?" After all, if you bought only government bonds, you would have a guaranteed income without having to cope with the ups and downs associated with the risk of ownership. Figure 4.1 answers that question for us.

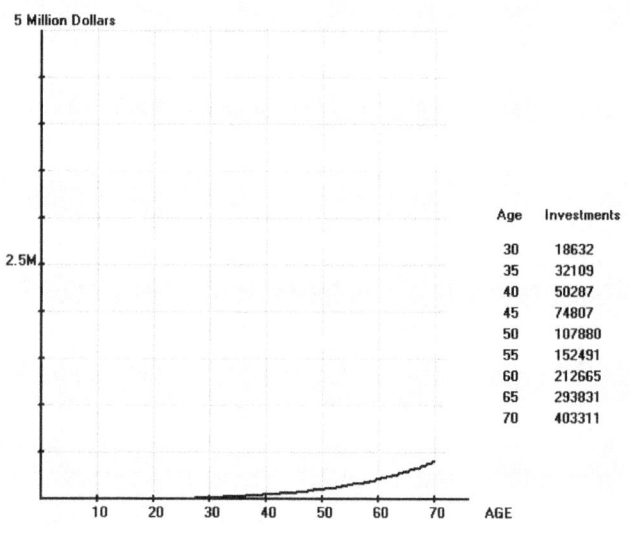

Age	Investments
30	18632
35	32109
40	50287
45	74807
50	107880
55	152491
60	212665
65	293831
70	403311

Figure 4.1: One hundred dollars a month grows slowly when invested at 6%.

Figure 4.1 assumes that you invest $100 each month in bonds earning 6%, starting at age 20. By age 70, you will have accumulated a little over $400,000. This is a lot of money, but compare this to the results from Figure 3.1 from the last chapter. In Figure 3.1 nearly everything was the same as the situation depicted by Figure 4.1. In both cases $100 a month was saved starting at age 20. In Figure 3.1 though, the money was assumed to be invested at 10%, a reasonable long-term average for stocks. With stocks, at age 70, the accumulated wealth was nearly two million dollars. That's almost five times the amount accumulated over the same period with bonds earning 6%.

As you can see, assuming the risk of being an owner rather than a lender can pay huge benefits. Only you can decide if those benefits are worth the risk for you. Before you decide though, you might want to fully understand what the risks are, and how they can be minimized.

The graphs of Figures 3.1 and 4.1 are smooth and show a steady growth. In the real world this is seldom the case. Historically, for example, if you had invested in stocks over a typical forty-year period you would have had gains in only about thirty of those years. In each of the other ten years, you would have had losses averaging about 10% of your total investment. In very bad years, your investment might have dropped as much as 20%. This erratic movement of stock prices is to be expected. If you don't fully understand this movement, it is easy to loose money if you invest in stocks.

In order to understand the price fluctuations, we first need a way to determine the "true" value of a share of stock. There are many ways to approach this subject. For example, we might total all the assets for the company and divide that amount by the number of outstanding shares. While this is not an unreasonable approach, it usually is not the best method for determining the value of a company. It only shows how much the company is worth if you were to cease the business and sell off the assets.

A method of evaluation that works reasonably well is to base the value of a company on the amount of profit it will provide to you in the foreseeable future. The more income a stock can generate for you, the more you should be willing to pay for that stock. If we divide a company's total yearly profit by the number of outstanding shares, we get the earnings generated per share of stock. If we divide the price of a share by the earnings per share, we get a number referred to as the P/E ratio (Price divided by Earnings). The P/E allows investors to compare the "value" of two similar companies easily. For sake of example, assume two hotel chains have P/E's of 10 and 20 respectively. If all other factors are equal, the hotel chain with a P/E of 10 is a much better value because you only have to spend $10 to buy an income stream of $1/year. The company with a P/E of 20 will give you the same income, but it will cost you $20.

You should not try to compare the P/E ratios for dissimilar companies such as a brand new clothing retailer and a well-established hotel chain. Since different industries have different risks, comparing P/E ratios only makes sense when the companies are comparable. It is appropriate though, to compare a specific company's P/E to its industry average to see how it stacks up. Perhaps you are wondering what a reasonable P/E is for a company.

To answer that question, let's look at the P/E for something easy to evaluate like a bond. If we assume a bond that pays a 5% coupon, its P/E would be 20 because you would have to invest $20 to get $1 of interest. If a company made enough profit to pay its stockholders a 5% return, we might expect a similar P/E for that company. Unfortunately it's not that easy. Suppose, for example, that a fictitious company makes the majority of its profits from manufacturing photographic film for 35mm cameras. They might be generating a 5% return today, but if you think digital cameras are going to dominate the industry in the future, you might not be willing to invest unless the P/E was much lower (meaning that you get a larger return on your money).

On the other hand, imagine that a film company is not making much profit today because more and more people are using digital cameras. But if you read that the company is re-tooling many of its plants so they can produce photographic paper for inkjet printers, you might expect that the company's profits will be much larger in the near future. Based on this scenario, you might be willing to pay much more for the stock that it is worth based on its *current* P/E.

The above discussion may seem very complicated but it can be summarized easily. The true value of a company is not based on its current earnings, but on its *expected* earnings in the future. This is why a new company that has never had even one dollar of profit might command a large stock price. People that believe there will be huge profits later will be willing to pay more now than a company's current P/E indicates that it is worth. They base their evaluation of the company's worth on its future (expected) earnings. The fact that two reasonable people might make different predictions about a company's future earnings is one reason why stock prices fluctuate.

The amount someone is willing to pay for a stock certainly is affected by that person's estimation of the actual value of the company, but at any given point in time, there are many other factors. If a person is worried about war and terrorism in the world, for example, the fact that they feel uneasy might make them not want to take the risk of investing their money. It is important to realize that it makes no difference if their fears are based on actual fact or not. If they are worried, for any reason, the worry alone could prevent them from investing their money. It could even make them sell some of the investments they have and use that money to buy less risky investments such as bonds.

The point is this. At any point in time there will be people that think a certain company is overvalued and others that think it is undervalued based on their perceptions of the economy, their personal problems, their predictions for the company's future earnings, etcetera. When the number of people that think the price of a company is overvalued is equal to the number that think it is undervalued, the price of a company's stock will be stable. Otherwise, it will change. Let's see why.

One of the wonderful things about the major stock markets is that there is always a buyer if you want to sell your stock and there is always stock available if you decide you want to purchase some. The actual process that allows for this to happen can vary from one stock exchange to another, but let's look at a simplified example that can provide a realistic overview.

Assume for a moment that someone we will call Mr. Smith owns a *seat* on the New York Stock Exchange. It would be Mr. Smith's responsibility to make-a-market for the stocks of a particular company, and as part of that responsibility, Mr. Smith will be required to own a substantial amount of shares of that company. Whenever someone wants to purchase some shares, Mr. Smith will sell them some. If someone wants to sell the shares they own, Mr. Smith will buy them. Obviously, Mr. Smith would prefer not to deplete the number of shares of stock he owns by selling them all to others. He also would not want to end up with too many shares of stock by buying the shares people want to sell. How can he solve this problem?

The basis for a solution is easy to understand. Mr. Smith could maintain a constant number of personally owned shares if the number of shares that people want to buy is the same as the number of shares that people want to sell. Mr. Smith can force this to happen by simply changing the price of the stock. Let's look at an example.

Assume Mr. Smith makes a market in XYZ Company stock. Also assume that the stock is currently selling for $20 a share and that the number of buyers is equal to the number of sellers. Everything seems fine, but let's add a twist. Suppose XYZ Company has a lot of delivery trucks. Also assume that the price of oil and gasoline has been rising. If the people that own XYZ stock decide the company is not going to make as much profit this year because of increases in fuel costs, some of the people might decide to sell some or all of their XYZ stock.

Mr. Smith is obligated to buy their stock, but remember, he needs to turn around and sell those to other buyers in order to keep his personal inventory of XYZ stock from growing or shrinking. Since prospective buyers also know that XYZ might not be making as much profit this year, they will not be overly interested in purchasing XYZ stock, at least not at its current price. So Mr. Smith lowers the price of the stock from $20 a share to $19. This helps in two ways.

At the lower price of $19 a share, more people will want to buy XYZ stock, even if they think the profits will be lower. Perhaps they calculate that higher gasoline prices will only cut XYZ's profits by 2%. When they compare this with the 5% drop in the price, they might think XYZ is a bargain because they believe its future P/E will improve. Or, they might think the price of oil will be going back down soon or maybe they believe XYZ will cut costs somewhere else and keep profits close to what they have been, again boosting the P/E. Regardless of the reason though, the point is valid. When the price of a stock goes down, more people will want to purchase it at the new price than would have bought it at the old price.

This is not really a complex idea. We see similar situations all the time. If your local grocery store, for example, has bananas on sale for 60 cents a pound, and not enough people are buying them, then the store will lower the price. They have no real alternative. They can't just let the bananas set there and go bad. They must ensure that the number of buyers is equal to the number of bananas.

The same is true for Mr. Smith. If he needs more people to buy the stock (because there are more people that want to sell than want to buy) then he must lower the price. It was stated earlier that lowering the price helped in two ways, so let's look at the second way.

When the price of XYZ stock is lowered, some of the people that were planning to sell it for $20 (the price it was yesterday) might decide they will just keep it if they can only get $19 per share. Thus we see that lowering the price of the stock not only increases the number of buyers, it can also decrease the number of sellers. If, after lowering the price, Mr. Smith finds that there are still more sellers than buyers, he will have to lower the price again. In fact, he will continue to lower the price until the number of sellers and buyers are equal.

Just the opposite happens if the number of buyers is greater than the number of sellers. Suppose that XYZ announces they are buying a new fleet of trucks with much better gas mileage and that they expect their profits to increase next year. In order to keep the number of buyers and sellers equal, Mr. Smith will need to increase the price of XYZ stock.

It is in Mr. Smith's best interest to monitor the number of sellers and buyers of XYZ stock closely and to constantly adjust the price of the stock not only daily but minute-by-minute or even second-by-second based on the volume of sales he handles. These adjustments made by the stock exchanges cause the price of stocks to fluctuate constantly.

You might have wondered how Mr. Smith gets paid for providing his services. There are really two prices Mr. Smith uses for stock. He has a *bid* price that he quotes to people that want to sell and an *ask* price for those that want to buy. In our example, the bid price might have been $19 and the ask price might have been $19.05. This would mean that Mr. Smith makes 5 cents for each share of stock he brokers. The difference between the bid and the ask prices varies based on the volume of shares traded.

You can see now that the price of a share of stock in XYZ Company can fluctuate because the company's current value is actually changing, but it can also fluctuate because investor's projections of future earnings can be influenced by both valid and invalid reasons. In the long run, the stock price for a given company should average its true value, but in the short run the value may be higher or lower than the true value.

Obviously, an investor would like to buy a stock when it is priced below its true value (or at least at a low price relative to its average) and then sell it sometime in the future for more than its true value. While this is certainly a worthwhile goal, historical data shows that it is not likely to happen, at least when it comes to typical investors. In fact, even trained stock market analysts often tend to break-even on their bets over time. By this I mean that although they have some very good years, their average is not any better than the market's average, especially after you deduct their fees. The good news is that you don't have to buy and sell at just the right time in order to make money in the stock market. In Chapter 5 we will explore this idea as well as various ways to reduce your risks.

Chapter 5
Reducing Risk

In Chapter 4 we compared owning stocks to owning bonds
in both risk and reward. As you recall, assuming the risk of
ownership increases the average rate of return from about
6% (bonds) to 10% (stocks). We saw that over a lifetime
of investing, a 4% difference in your return could increase
the total value of your investments by 400%.

Obviously, such a huge difference is worth taking some
risks. But what if we could get these magnificent gains
with very little risk? Not only is this possible, but it is
relatively easy to accomplish. The first step in
understanding how this can be achieved is to understand
why stock prices fluctuate and we learned that in the last
chapter. Now we are ready to explore ways to reduce the
risk associated with price fluctuations.

As you would expect, this reduction in risk does not
come without costs. Instead of trying to make the absolute
maximum profits, we can eliminate much of the risk by
simply being satisfied with the average return. If we truly
want to *maximize* our investment returns, we would need to
sell our stock when it reaches a short-term temporary high
from being overvalued. After the sale, we would wait
patiently as stock prices fell to a temporary low (from being
undervalued) where we would reinvest all of our
investment funds.

Unfortunately it is very difficult to determine the temporary highs and lows in advance. Perhaps, if the stock prices were always their "true" value, we could rely on mountains of mathematical calculations to determine exactly when to buy and sell. Such information would allow us to generate huge returns and many *technical analysts* make a living trying to predict the market fluctuations using mathematics.

While there are people that have been reasonably successful at predicting market fluctuations for relatively short periods of time, no one has ever come up with a formula or plan that works all the time. The reason of course is simple. We learned about it in the last chapter. The price of stocks is not based solely on the actual value they have at the moment. The price at any given time is based future predictions in earnings, current feelings of worry and exuberance, and many other factors far too complicated to be consistently envisioned

As we will see later, there are times when economic and social conditions might give us signals that we feel we can't ignore. In those rare cases, it might be justified to buy, sell, or alter some of our investments. In most cases, though, you will acquire very reasonable returns if you just buy a stock and hold it for a lengthy period of time. Let's revisit an example we used in Chapter 3 where we saw that investing $100 a month over a lifetime at an average return of 10% could yield $1,915,000. If you invested your $100 a month regardless of the state of the economy, you would purchase some shares at inflated prices and other shares at a bargain. Over an extended period of time, you would likely get the average return of 10%.

Instead of sticking to the plan of $100 each month, though, let's analyze what could happen if you decided to not invest when you think the market will do poorly and invest double when you think it will do well. If you guess right, your returns would be far greater than the 10%

average we are expecting. Unfortunately, in most cases, guesses are just that, guesses.

Most people that try to time-the-market are influenced by many factors, not the least of which is other's opinions. When they hear their friends and co-workers brag about how well they are doing in the market they want to share in their success, so they tend to increase their investments. When those around them are complaining about loosing money in the market, most people tend to stop investing and may even decide to sell some or all of the stocks they already own. Let's analyze this further.

If everyone around you is bragging about how much money they are making, you can probably bet that the market is at or approaching one of it peaks. This is when you should be selling, not buying. If everyone around you is complaining that they are loosing money, the market is probably in a slump, possibly near a temporary low. You should be buying not selling. Notice that this means that most people tend to buy when they should be selling and sell when they should be buying. This is a very important concept and I urge you to carefully read this paragraph and the last one again. As you start to understand, you'll begin to see why many investors loose money when investing in stocks.

When the market is doing poorly and everyone is complaining, many investors don't just stop buying, they sell some or all of the stocks they already own because they are scared of loosing more. History shows that markets rebound eventually, and often do so relatively quickly once the recovery starts. If you stay invested, and especially if you buy more stocks while prices are low, then you are able to participate in the recovery. Many people though, sell out when prices are low (so they loose money) and then buy back in only when the market is strong (and the prices are high again). Such behavior prevents them from making money when the market is recovering from its inevitable lows. At the next downturn panic sets in again and the cycle continues.

The moral is that if you try to time the market, you may find yourself buying high and selling low causing you to constantly loose money. Even if you are able to guess correctly part of the time, it is extremely unlikely that you will end up beating the market average. So why take so much risk? If you just invest *constantly over a long period of time*, you are almost 100% guaranteed that the market will return a reasonable average return.

The phrase of "long period of time" in the last paragraph is very important concept. Let's explore it by looking at an example. Suppose you have a friend that buys and sells classic automobiles and you have watched him make lots of money over the years. Let's also assume that your friend found a car in Florida that he wants to buy, but does not have the time to go and get it. Because the buyer won't take a check, your friend gives you a plane ticket, $10,000 in cash to pay for the car, and a little extra for your time and expenses.

You decide to take advantage of your free airline ticket and leave a few days early to spend some vacation time in the sun. During your vacation time in Florida, you just happen to come across an old Corvette that you can buy for only $7000. Since you have watched your friend buy and sell cars for years, you know the Corvette is worth at least $10,000, perhaps even double the asking price.

Knowing you have three days before you have to buy the car for your friend, you decide to use *his* money to buy the Corvette. It is such a good value, that you assume you can resell it for a nice profit for yourself and still buy your friend's car on schedule. After you buy the Corvette and try to sell it for a couple days though, you discover the entire area is filled with people that do not have the extra money or the desire to buy a classic car. You suspect that's why your friend was getting such a good deal on the car he was buying and why the Corvette you found was so reasonably priced.

You have no doubt that you got a good deal on the Corvette, and if you had *time* to advertise the car longer or take it to another area you could have made a nice profit. But because you must sell it quickly, you must deal with the buyers you have at the moment. By the end of the day you have to settle on a buyer with $6500 and have to use $500 of your own money to complete the deal for your friend. Let's analyze the risk you took when purchasing the Corvette and compare it to buying stocks.

The Corvette example shows that even if you have a quality investment you might loose money if you have to sell it on a fixed timetable. When you buy stocks the situation is the same. Even if you invest in a well-run company with a fantastic product you might loose money if you have to sell your stock soon after you buy it. Remember, the price of stock *over time* will reflect its real value. But, in the short run, many events can affect the price of the stock.

Perhaps a competitor announces a breakthrough that gives them the edge until your company can mount a counter offensive. Maybe something happens that's totally out of the company's control. Maybe the company is named in a lawsuit that could reduce their short-term profits. Perhaps there is a terrorist attack or a labor union is demanding higher wages. Any number of factors can send prices plummeting in the short run. Even if there is no merit to the lawsuit or the labor union is unlikely to strike, people may shy away from buying the stock. Remember, as we have discussed earlier, people don't always have to have a valid reason for not buying a particular product or stock in a particular company. Validity is not important. If there are less people wanting to buy than to sell for any reason, then the price will drop.

I could go on with example after example, but the point should be clear. The true value of a stock can fluctuate erratically for very valid, though often difficult-to-predict, reasons. The fluctuations from valid reasons can be enhanced and magnified by numerous invalid reasons. The good news is that even though such short-run fluctuations are nearly impossible to predict, the long-range behavior is generally foreseeable. This means you can reduce the risks associated with buying stock if you don't invest money that you will need in the short-term. More on this later.

Even though long-range behavior is easier to predict, it is important to realize that even long-range behavior is not totally predictable. Sometimes there are complications (such as competition, fraud, government regulations, war, the price of oil, etc.) that can erode or destroy a company without obvious warnings.

It is important to understand that any company, no matter how large or how profitable, may stumble or even fail. It is also important to realize that such failures are far from common. Even so, if our goal is to eliminate risk, we must find ways of handling any possible problem. The solution is not nearly as difficult as you might be imagining. Remember, even though any company might fail, most companies are successful, especially when evaluated over an extended period of time.

If we invest in ten or even fifty companies instead of only one, the odds of loosing money because one or two of them falters is greatly reduced. Furthermore, if we consistently buy stock in these companies on a monthly basis we eliminate the chance that we invest all of our money right before a huge downturn in the market. Additionally, if you continue to invest after a stock market crash, you will be buying your stocks at rock-bottom prices, giving you an extra boost as the market starts to rebound.

This means that you can reduce your risk in the stock market by investing consistently over an extended period of time, in a relatively large number of companies. If you do all three of these things, you can be virtually assured that you will achieve a 10% return (the historical average for stocks) on your investment. Unfortunately, most investors fail at one or more of these things. As we are about to see, they do so because they make poor choices in life.

I believe many people would make different choices if they only understood the alternatives available to them as well as the consequences of choosing those alternatives. Let's look at some practical ways to achieve the three requirements for eliminating investment risk. First let's itemize the three requirements.

- You must invest over an *extended* period of time. This means starting as early as possible so that you have the longest possible time frame. The longer the period, the more your investments will grow because of compounding and the less your risk will be because you have time to smooth out short-run fluctuations.

- You must invest *consistently*. This means you cannot stop investing when times are tough, and even more important, you must not sell investments you already own when the market is in a slump.

- You must *spread* your investment dollars over a wide range of companies so that you can achieve the market average over time. This also allows you to eliminate the catastrophic consequences of having a significant percentage of your money invested in a company that files for bankruptcy.

The first of these requirements was discussed at length in Chapter 1, 2 and 3. To achieve this goal only requires that you decide that wealth in the long-run is worth giving up some things in the short-run. You can give up a lot for a very short time, or give up a little over your entire life. What you give up and for how long is entirely up to you. The software discussed in Chapter 9 will help you compare the consequences of a wide variety of choices so you can decide what approach is right for you.

The second of these requirements may seem difficult, but it's only a matter of being properly prepared. Remember the Corvette example. If you had purchased the Corvette with your own money, you could have taken as long as needed to sell the car. In the same vein, you should never invest money in the stock market that you might need in the short-run. For example, if you have saved $10,000 to send your daughter to college next year, you should not use it to buy stocks. As we have discussed, at any point in time (such as one year from now) the market may be up or down. If the market is down and you must sell stock to pay the tuition, then your loses are final.

On the other hand, it makes sense to start investing in stocks for your newly born daughter's education if you have 18 years before she will need the money. The market will have its ups and downs, but if you consistently purchase stock in a variety of companies, the long-range trends will reward you with profits.

Let's revisit the idea that you must ensure that you never have to sell when the market is down. On the surface, that sounds like a difficult problem. Actually, all you have to do is make sure you always have enough money available to handle life's short-run requirements and disasters. This simply means you should not invest all of your money in the stock market. You should keep enough money in cash to handle the "unexpected" things you know you have to expect. Things like tires for your car and a plane ticket to see a sick relative fall in this category. You many not know exactly when such things will happen, but it is predictable that, given enough time, they will happen.

You should also be prepared for less likely, but still very possible, disasters such as loosing your job or a major repair on your car. If these types of problems occur when the market is in a slump you are penalized twice. You have to sell more of your stock to get the money you need (because it is worth less in a slump) and you won't have as much invested when the market recovers. The amount of money you need in reserve to handle such situations will vary based on such things as age, lifestyle, education, and marital status. Perhaps a reasonable amount for a typical person would be three month's salary, but others might need more.

Part of this money should be kept in a checking account (one that pays interest if possible) so that it is available at a moment's notice. The rest can be in a savings account or even short-term bonds where even more interest can be earned. None of these investments will give you as much return as stocks, in the long run, but they allow you to eliminate the risk on the money you do invest in the market.

Let's look at what this means. When you start to save, you should first create a financial safety net that can handle the expenses and disasters that come to everyone in life. Then, and only then, should you begin to invest in stocks. Unfortunately, many people become greedy even if they have this philosophy to begin with. After they have a few years of successful investing they decide the market is always going to go up. They slowly move all of their funds into stocks to get bigger returns only to loose big when a market downturn forces them to sell stocks at the worst possible time.

Remember, the market can give you an average return of 10% only if you can leave the money invested long enough to achieve the average. A good rule of thumb based on historical data, indicates that you should not invest any money that you might need in less than five years. As stated earlier, the amount you personally need in reserve depends on many factors. For example, you might be willing and able to take on a part-time job to obtain extra cash when unexpected situations occur. Others might have family obligations that would prohibit such an option. The possible alternatives are different for everyone, but if you understand the consequences for the choices you have, then you can decide what is best for you.

The third requirement for eliminating risk was to spread your investment among many different companies, perhaps fifty or more. There is actually a very easy way of doing this. Instead of buying stocks in individual companies, you can invest in mutual funds. Even though mutual funds are actually very easy to buy and sell, you can make better choices if you understand all the options available to you. The next chapter is devoted entirely to mutual funds and similar financial instruments.

It was mentioned earlier that you could invest your needed reserves in bonds in order to get a higher return than a savings account. There are risks associated with bonds that should be discussed in this chapter. Many people think that high quality bonds or government treasuries are risk free. If you hold a bond to maturity, you will get back the face value of the bond. If you have to sell a bond before its maturity date though, you face considerable risk. Let's look at some examples to demonstrate this point.

Assume you buy a $1000 bond paying the current interest rate of 5% for 10 years. After owning the bond for only a year though you decide you need the cash. During that year, assume the interest on new bonds rises to 7%. If you try to sell your 5% bond now, potential buyers have a choice. If they buy your bond, it will only pay them $50 a year in interest. If they buy a new $1000 bond, they will get $70 a year. There is no question that they will prefer the new bond over yours. The only way you can get them to buy your bond is to sell it to them at a discount.

Hopefully this simple example shows how you can loose money on bonds if you have to sell them before their maturity date. In much the same manner, you can make money if you sell bonds during a period of declining interest rates. The point is that bonds are not nearly as risk free as most people believe. As with stocks though, there are ways that we can reduce the risks associated with bonds.

We can eliminate bond risk by not putting ourselves in a situation where we have to sell a bond (just like we never want to be in a position where we must sell our stocks). One way to do this would be to only buy very short-term bonds. Unfortunately, short-term bonds generally do not pay nearly as much interest as long-term bonds. The solution is to *ladder* your bonds. Laddering, simply means to buy bonds with various maturity dates so that you are constantly having bonds mature when you might need them. Let's see how this works.

Let's assume you know you are going to need $10,000 a year for the next 5 years. You realize that the stock market is not a good place to keep the $50,000 you will need because a temporary downturn could force you to sell at a loss. In order to get the highest possible interest rates, you buy five $10,000 bonds with maturities of one, two, three, four, and five years. This ensures that the money will be available when you need it, and it allows you to mix some short-term bonds with slightly longer-term bonds to give you a better average rate of return.

Let's alter the above example slightly to demonstrate another point. Suppose you have a situation where you *might* need $10,000 each year and you want to ensure that it is available should the need arise, but unless problems come up, you think you can get by without it. First, ladder the bonds as described above. Then, as each bond matures (assuming you don't need the cash that year) you can use the proceeds from the sale of that bond to buy another 5-year bond.

At the end of the first year you replace the 1-year bond with a 5-year. The next year you replace the 2-year with another 5-year. You keep this up until you have five 5-year bonds. This way all of your money is eventually invested in 5-year bonds while ensuring that the $10,000 you might need for emergencies becomes available each year. When used properly, bonds can ensure you have emergency cash when you need it so that you never have to sell stocks when you don't want to.

So far in this chapter, we have discussed the idea of reducing the risks associated with investing in stocks and bonds. Unfortunately there are many *other* risks in life that threaten your financial security. The simple solution to these problems is insurance, but most people don't understand how to use insurance effectively. To illustrate the point, let's look at some proper and improper ways of using insurance.

Nearly every college graduate is bombarded with offers for life insurance. If they pursue any of these offers, they are given a well-organized sales pitch that shows how they can contribute to a whole-life policy for fifteen years or so and then get free life insurance forever. What they are not told is that the insurance company uses a small amount of their premiums to buy *term* insurance (and term insurance is cheap when you are young) and invests the rest. The value of these investments compounds over time, creating enough money to continue paying for term insurance as well as generating a lifetime of profits for the insurance company.

You can easily do this for yourself (buy a term policy and invest the difference) but before you do, let's examine when and if you really need insurance. Insurance, with minor exceptions, should *only* be purchased to *prevent disasters*. Let's look at some examples to demonstrate the point.

Suppose you are single, no children, and just out of college. If you were to die, there is *no* disaster. Obviously dying is not a great thing from your point of view, but if you have no family to support, there is no disaster, and therefore no reason for someone young and single to own life insurance. Ten years later, things might have changed. Perhaps you have a spouse and two kids. If you die at that point, there is a disaster. If you are the husband or working mother, your paycheck will be missed. If you are a stay-at-home mom or dad, how will your spouse pay for childcare and house cleaning if you die? These are the makings of real disasters.

Rather than purchase insurance you don't need when you are young, consider the consequences of adding what you would be paying in premiums to your investment plan. By the time you need insurance, you might have enough money to *not* need insurance. At the very least, you can probably get by with term insurance until your investments can provide the security your family needs.

Does this mean that someone young and single does not need insurance? No, it just means they generally don't need life insurance. What is needed is both *health* and *disability* insurance. Assume you are young and single and acquire a debilitating disease or have an accident that takes away your sight. Such situations could prevent you from working and with no spouse to take care of you, your life could certainly be a disaster.

Suppose you are driving a car that you can't afford to replace if it were totaled in an accident. Would it be a disaster if you were unable to get to work? Sure it would. That's why you have car insurance. But what if you drive an older car because you are putting every penny into your investment plan. You have enough money to easily replace the old car, so there is no disaster if you should happen to loose it. Therefore, you should consider not insuring the car itself. But, if you run your old car into a brand new Mercedes, and have to pay the owner $100,000 to replace his car, you have a disaster. Even if you have that much in your portfolio, it is a disaster to have years of investing destroyed by a simple accident, so you should purchase liability insurance to pay for damages you might cause others. (Besides, liability insurance is required by law.)

As you can see, there are very valid reasons for owning insurance. No matter how much money you have, it is a disaster if you have to replace a house that burns down. If you have a million dollars and someone slips on your sidewalk they can see you as a target. An *umbrella* policy that protects you in such cases is cheap insurance when compared to the potential disasters that you face. Everyone that has accumulated wealth should ask their insurance agent about an umbrella policy.

When you are confronted with any situation where insurance may be necessary, just look for the disaster. If one is apparent, then by all means purchase insurance. If you can't see a true disaster though, assume the risk yourself and invest what you would have spent on premiums.

Chapter 6
Mutual Funds and Similar Alternatives

Chapter 5 indicated that mutual funds could help eliminate risk in the market by allowing you to spread your investment over many different companies. In this chapter, you will not only see how that works, but you will also see how to reduce risk even further by using a variety of mutual funds (and similar instruments) to increase diversification. Furthermore, this chapter will explore ways to increase returns and reduce risk even further by buying and selling without emotion. Let's start by defining what a mutual fund is.

A mutual fund is simply a financial structure that allows many different investors to combine their money into a single pool so they can buy a wider variety of companies. Let's assume, for example, that you are investing $100 each month. Such a sum would allow you to buy only a few shares of a typical company. This is undesirable for two reasons.

First, the commissions paid for purchasing such a small amount of stock would be very high compared to the amount you are investing. The cost of doing a trade might be $25 (more or less depending on whether you use a discount or full-service broker) no matter how many shares you buy. If you invest $100, you are paying a 25%

commission whereas $25 is only .25% of a $10,000 purchase. The second reason that a small investment is undesirable is that the small amount of money prevents you from buying stock in many different companies.

With a mutual fund, you and thousands of other people contribute monthly payments (most companies have ways of reducing or eliminating initial required minimums). When these contributions are combined there can be enough money to buy blocks of stock in many different companies, thus solving both of the afore-mentioned problems. There are thousands of mutual funds available through banks, brokerage firms, as well as companies such as Vanguard or Fidelity that specialize in funds.

If you already have a lot of money to invest, it is possible to make much larger returns by investing in individual companies rather than in a mutual fund. Unfortunately, such a strategy also opens you to large losses if even one of your choices happens to be wrong. Mutual funds generally are a much better choice for young investors.

You can find toll-free phone numbers and Internet addresses for dozens of mutual fund companies in the ads of any investment magazine on the shelves of your local bookstore or supermarket. In general, mutual fund companies offer lower prices and more choices than banks and brokerage firms, but banks and brokerage firms argue that they provide more services. After reading the rest of this chapter, I hope you feel like you can make intelligent choices without having to pay for additional services.

A typical mutual fund has a manager that oversees research on the companies owned by the fund as well as those being considered for purchase. After studying the research data, the manager will decide what companies to buy and what companies to sell. If the manager and his or her research team does a good job, the fund will generate an above average return for you and others that own shares in the fund.

Some funds have an up-front commission called a *load*. Typical loads can be as high as 5% of your investment. In general, there is no reason to pay up front fees to invest your money. There are far too many unloaded funds available. It can be argued that commissions are required so that the best managers can be acquired, but a manager has to be consistently better to make up for the money lost to commissions, fees, and salaries.

All funds charge fees to cover the normal day-to-day expenses involved in running a fund. These yearly expenses vary from about .2% to over 1% of the money you have invested in the fund. If a fund charged .5% each year, and if they averaged the market return of 10.5%, then you would end up with a 10% return. Obviously, all things being equal, you want to invest in funds with the smallest fees.

The reason there are so many different funds available is that there are many different philosophies driving the investment strategies of different funds. As we look at the different types of funds available we will examine some of these investment strategies. As we will see, there are funds available for every possible investment philosophy. Don't be intimidated by all the choices available. By the end of this chapter, you will see strategies that will help you decide what funds are right for you.

Some funds invest in small companies while others invest in midsize or large companies. In general, larger companies are more stable (less risk), but smaller companies have the potential for bigger gains (as well as bigger losses). If you buy a *Large Cap* fund, for example, the fund's charter will require that only large companies that exceed a specified size be considered for purchase. A *Small Cap* or *Mid Cap* fund, on the other hand, will only invest in small or mid-sized companies. Mutual fund companies will send you a free prospectus outlining their investment philosophy and expenses for any fund they offer.

Small vs. large stocks is only one of many ways to distinguish a fund's philosophy. Many of the philosophies have overlapping characteristics, so don't expect each fund to be totally unique in its methodology. Another philosophies used by funds are *growth, income,* or *value.* Let's examine each of these in turn.

Growth stocks are generally small or mid-sized companies. They are classified as growth stocks because they are growing at a much faster rate than typical companies. Many growth companies are very profitable. Some growth companies though, are not yet making profits and those that are, can be making far less than larger more established companies. Often the growth itself (the cost of building new stores and increasing inventory, for example) is the reason for low profits.

You will find that most growth companies do not pay dividends to their stockholders. This is certainly understandable if the company is just starting up and not yet making a profit but it also makes sense even if the company is very profitable. If a company is growing at 20% a year, for example, it does not make sense to give the profits to the stockholders and then go out and borrow the money needed to expand. In the long run, it would be far more beneficial for the stockholders of a fast-growing company if dividends are retained to finance growth.

Income stocks, on the other hand, are usually large well-established companies that pay consistent dividends. Unlike a growth-fund where owners expect to make their profits from larger-than-average long-range appreciation in the price of the stocks, income fund owners expect to reap most of their returns from immediate dividends and a relatively small amount from long-range price gains.

In a market downturn, the prices of growth stocks often fall faster than the prices of dividend paying stocks. The reason is not hard to understand. When a stock is paying a dividend it has real value right now. The stock price of a growth company is based heavily on projected future earnings so even a hint of bad economic times can often send their stock price tumbling. Conversely, good news can temporarily push the price of a growth stock far above its true value. The point is that you should generally expect far more volatility from a growth fund than an income fund. The long-range average return of a growth fund is often large enough to make it worth the risk, but you have to be prepared, both financially and emotionally, to handle a roller coaster ride of price fluctuations.

Value stocks are those that are viewed as being priced below their true market value. A good example is a company whose stock price is temporarily down because of some dramatic but short-lived bad news. Or perhaps a company is just overlooked by investors for a short period of time causing the stock price to fall. Maybe an officer in the company is charged with a crime and the bad publicity temporarily drives potential buyers away. Perhaps a company has a one-time expense, such as remodeling all their stores, that drives down current profits even though sales are expected to improve in the long run. In all of these cases, the current stock price might be lower than the true value. Value fund managers use many methods for finding such companies.

Many funds specialize in a specific sector of the market. A technology fund, for example, would only invest in technology stocks. Some funds are even more specialized. A communication fund, for example, would only invest in technology companies that had some connection with the communication industry. These could include companies that manufacture telephones or companies that install microwave antennas or companies that provide Internet services, just to name a few.

Sector funds do not have to be based on products or services. Sometimes they are geographically based. There are, for example, European funds, Pacific Basin funds, and even funds for a particular country such as a Japanese fund. You can even find funds that invest only in certain geographical areas of the United States.

There are two other types of funds that should be mentioned. The first of these is *index* funds, but unlike a mutual fund, they do not have a high-paid manager that selects the stocks to purchase. Instead, a computer program coordinates buy and sell orders to make the fund track a particular market average such as the 500 or the 5000 largest companies in the United States. The advantage of an index fund is cost. Since they do not have the cost of a high-paid manager, the expenses for an index fund can often be as low as .2%, a full percentage point below many actively managed funds.

Consider that if you invest in an index fund that tracks the entire stock market, you should expect to receive an average return of 10.3% (the market average of 10.5% less a .2% expense fee). In order to beat this return using a managed fund with an expense of 1.2%, the manager would have to achieve an average return of 11.5%. Historically, this is unlikely. Sure, a manager might beat the market one or even several years in a row, but the risks taken to beat the market in good times often cause above average losses in bad years. Rather than take on more risk, many people choose to invest some or all of their portfolio in index funds.

Another type of fund is called an ETF or *exchange-traded-funds*. When you buy or sell shares in a typical mutual fund, the actual transaction takes place at the end of the business day. Assume for a moment, that the market is up one morning and you decide to sell a portion of a fund you own. Even though you placed the order that morning, the market could move to a lower position throughout the afternoon and net you less cash from your sale than you had expected. ETFs are traded like stocks, allowing buy and sell transactions to take place immediately. Since they are traded like stocks though, ETFs are subject to normal transaction commissions making them less attractive for those investing relatively small amounts of money each month. When you are young and investing small amounts each month you will have lower costs if you use standard mutual funds and index funds. Later in life, when you have accumulated significant wealth, you can consider ETFs or even individual stocks.

There are even mutual funds for investments other than stocks. A REIT (Real Estate Investment Trust) for example, invests its funds in various types of real estate. Some REITs specialize in commercial ventures while other deal with residential projects.

There are a variety of bond funds available too. For example, you can purchase a fund that specializes in short-term government bonds, corporate bonds, or even junk bonds (high risk, high return bonds).

The large variety of bond funds, mutual funds, index funds, ETFs, and REITs available, provides you with many choices. Let's look at ways of utilizing these financial tools in your investment plan.

Suppose you feel strongly that companies involved in health care are going to do especially well over the next decade as the baby boomers grow older. Even though you feel confident about this, you might not have the expertise to determine *which* companies are most likely to perform the best or you might not have enough money to buy enough different health care companies to reduce your risk. If you buy a health care fund, you solve both these problems. The fund management team would do the appropriate research and buy companies that appear to have the best chance for success. The fund would also own many health-oriented companies, giving you a safety net if several of the companies happen to perform poorly for some unexpected reason.

If you mix funds of different investment strategies (value, income, growth, small cap, large cap, etc.) you have the potential to minimize fluctuations in your total investment portfolio. Historically, for example, you could have invested all your money in just Growth funds and averaged about 10%. Similarly, if you had chosen to buy only Value funds, your average return would still be about 10%. For short periods of time, perhaps even as long as a decade, one type of fund may perform much better than another, but in the long-run there is very little difference.

In the long run, if you spread your investment dollars among several types of funds, your average returns should equal the average for the entire market, but probably with less fluctuation in the year-to-year value of your investments. This is a very beneficial byproduct of *diversifying* your investment dollars among various types of investments.

The reason for less fluctuation is not hard to understand. Based on economic conditions, current tax laws, international competition, and many other factors, different types of companies will do well during different periods of time. Small companies might have a growth spurt for a few years and then level off while corporate giants have their day. Perhaps domestic stocks surge while foreign stocks lag for a few years only to have the situation reversed for a similar period of time.

Having your portfolio balanced with various types of funds can help you achieve your goals while adding stability because the value of some of your investments might increase while others are decreasing. Having a variety of funds can also help you beat the average return if you are willing to do a little work each year. Let's look at an example to see how this could work.

Let's assume you invest $200 each month with a mutual fund company such as Vanguard or Fidelity and that you have the money equally divided into five funds, perhaps a domestic total market index fund, an emerging markets foreign fund, a large-cap fund, a value fund, and an energy fund. Let's also assume that after a few years of investing, the total value of your funds has grown to $10,000. Since you invested equally in each fund, you might expect each to have a value of approximately $2000. When you examine your financial statement though, let's assume you find the following values.

Total market index fund	$1,950
Emerging market foreign fund	2,420
Large-cap fund	1,580
Value fund	2,100
Energy fund	1,840

From these figures, we can see that foreign stocks are doing very well, while large domestic companies and energy companies are struggling. The reasons for the varying results, especially in hindsight, might be easy to understand. Perhaps expansion of foreign economies is hurting the sales of large US companies. Maybe the energy sector is taking a hit because automakers have been required by the government to offer expensive hybrid engines in 50% of the cars they produce. For whatever reason, different aspects of the world's economy are progressing at different rates.

Regardless of past performance though, it is unlikely that future performance will be the same. The sectors that are doing poorly will find ways to cut cost or otherwise increase their competitiveness and industries that are doing extremely well draw new competition. Let's use this concept along with an understanding of human nature to see why some people make money in the market and others don't.

Assume we have two people that are each in the investment situation described above. Let's call them Mr. X and Mr. Y. Mr. X looks at the totals for his funds and decides that he is making much more money in foreign stocks so he sells his other funds and invests it all in various foreign funds. Over the next few years, the world economy does indeed change and the foreign stocks either loose money or barely hold their own. Meanwhile, domestic stocks, especially the large companies finally get their act together and enjoy several years of above average profits.

Mr. X again analyzes how his investments are doing and decides to sell all his foreign stocks and concentrate on large US companies. If this trend continues we see Mr. X constantly shifting his money to the funds that performed well *last* year. This means he often buys into sectors of the market that are at their peak, which generally means his investments are eventually subjected to an inevitable decline or at least not fairing as well as other choices he could have made. Let's compare his strategies with that of Mr. Y.

Mr. Y understands the concepts we have discussed and realizes that the fluctuations of the market are normal, and expects them to average out over time. When his portfolio has become unbalanced, he buys and sells, not to chase last year's winners, but to *return his percentages in each fund to his original objectives*. This simply means he sell some of the funds that are doing well and reinvests those dollars in funds whose values are down in order to make sure the value of each fund has been returned to 20% of his total investment (equal amounts in each fund).

By regaining his original percentages, Mr. Y *balances* his portfolio. Notice that this action forces him to sell some of the stocks he owns that are doing the best, stocks that might well be at their peaks. He is also forced to buy stocks that are down, stocks that are effectively on sale. The best part is that he can perform this action based solely on mathematics. He objectively ensures that 20% of his available investment dollars are allocated to each of his five funds. This is very different from the emotional buying and selling done by Mr. X.

When we make decisions based primarily on emotion, we have a good chance of being disappointed with the long-range outcomes of those decisions. This is why it is so important to understand the basic concepts of investing. If we know the options available to us and the most likely consequences associated with those options, we have a much better chance of making choices that are right for us.

It was mentioned earlier that you should have a diversified mix of funds in your portfolio. A reasonable mix would include foreign and domestic funds as well as exposure to small, medium and large companies and perhaps a REIT. You may want to include different investment strategies such as growth, income, and value. If you have many years before retirement, you should consider taking more risk with a portion of your portfolio by investing in emerging growth funds (new companies) or specific sectors that you are confident in. A truly balanced portfolio might have both managed funds and index funds.

Most financial experts dictate that you should carry a percentage of bonds in your portfolio mix. A common rule-of-thumb that is often quoted is that your percentage of bonds should be equal to your age. Such generic rules may have some validity, but I think it makes more sense to use the philosophy discussed earlier. Keep enough money in bonds and a savings account to handle your all your short and medium term needs and emergencies and keep the rest invested in stocks to give you the maximum possible return over time. That way, the amount you invest in bonds is correct for your specific situation. Of course, as your situations change (your age, having children, worries about employment, etcetera) you need to adjust your bond reserves to handle your particular needs.

Just as you want to make sure you have a reasonable amount of diversity, it is also important to limit the amount of funds you have to perhaps ten or so. If you get much more than that, you probably could just buy one total-market fund and achieve the same results with less hassles. In most cases though, the advantages of balancing your percentages is worth the hassle.

The actual mix you choose is not nearly as important as balancing everything back to your original percentages on a regular basis. It is important not to get obsessive about balancing. If you balanced every month, for example, the normal market fluctuations could have you moving money between funds all the time, costing you both time and money. Instead, establish an easy to remember date (such as your birthday), to check the balance of your portfolio. If the fund percentages are *significantly* skewed, return them to their original percentages. If not, leave them alone.

Chapter 7
Taxes

Even if you currently have a modest income and fall in a low tax bracket, this information in this chapter applies to you. As we saw in the early chapters, even a modest investment plan of $100 a month can build your wealth into the millions. When your investment grows, so does the income generated. A million dollars, for example, could easily generate $100,000 or more in income during a good year. Add that to the income from your job and you can easily find yourself paying forty percent or more of your income in state and federal taxes.

The effect that taxes have on a long-term investment plan can be enormous. Lowering the expected average return from 10% to 6% (40% going to taxes) can decrease the value of a $100 a month investment from $1.9 million to $403,000 over a lifetime. Reducing your taxes has exactly the same effect as increasing your returns. This implies that you should put the same effort into tax planning as you put into boosting your pretax returns.

Taxes also reduce the amount you have to invest initially. Always remember, it's not how much income you make, it's how much you get to keep. In this chapter, we will explore ways of reducing, postponing, and eliminating taxes. Taxes may seem complicated, but as with everything else, if you understand the consequences of the options available to you, the decisions almost make themselves. Some of the options to be discussed are potential choices for nearly everyone. Other options will apply only to people in certain situations. You should also keep in mind that tax laws are continually being changed so you should verify the appropriateness of any tactic you are considering.

Let's start with some ideas that can be utilized by nearly everyone. If you buy a stock and sell that stock *within a year*, any profits you make are classified as a *short-term gain* and generally taxed as normal income, which means at the highest possible rates. The profits from the sale of stocks held for *more than a year* are considered *long-term gains* and are generally taxed at a much lower rate. This means that you can reduce the taxes on your investment gains by making sure you hold a stock at least twelve months before you sell it.

This same rule does not apply directly to a mutual fund. Even if you buy a fund and hold it longer than a year you may be subject to short-term gains. This is true because the gains and losses of the fund are based on the individual stocks traded by the mutual fund company itself. Very aggressive funds often buy stocks and trade them quickly, thus creating short-term gains. The prospectus for a fund provides information about expected tax consequences for that fund.

There are funds that are specifically designed to be tax-friendly because they try to hold the stocks they buy for at least a year if not much longer. If you hold a stock for 10 years, for example, the company can grow year after year without any tax consequences from the appreciating stock value. You only become subject to the tax when you finally sell the stock. Another attribute of tax friendly funds can be to buy companies that pay significant dividends, which are currently taxed at a lower rate than normal income. (Always check the *current* tax laws.)

If you prefer to bypass the higher expenses of a managed fund, you can still postpone your taxes. Index funds, by their very nature, are tax friendly. Since an index fund mimics the current market proportions, it rarely has to make any significant changes to its makeup. This means less buys and sells, which means less tax consequences for holders of the fund.

If you work for a company that offers a 401K plan, it should be a major part of your investment strategy. A 401K plan allows you to contribute about 15% of your income (the actual amount can vary based on a variety of factors) annually to the plan. One great thing is that these contributions are made before taxes are calculated for your income. This essentially means that the government is subsidizing your savings plan.

Suppose you are in a 20% tax bracket and you are contributing $100 each month into the plan. Since your income will be effectively reduced by $100 each month, your taxes will be reduced by 20% of that $100. That means your paycheck only drops by $80 for each $100 you save. This is like getting an immediate 25% return on your money. But it gets even better.

Nearly all companies that offer 401K plans to their employees match some portion of the employee's contributions. The amount of match varies considerably, but let's assume, for sake of example, that a company matches the first 5% of your contributions. Let's also assume that you are making $30,000 a year and that you are contributing 10% of your income to the plan and that you are in a 20% tax bracket. This means that your total contribution would be $3000 a year even though your paycheck would only drop by $2400. Furthermore, since the company is matching half of your 10%, your yearly savings rises by another $1500.

But it still gets better. Most companies with 401K plans share a portion of their profits each year with their employees *that participate in the plan*. Employees that don't participate loose out. This profit sharing contribution can add hundreds of dollars to your account each year. Totaling all these benefits means you can add perhaps $4800 or more each year to your plan while your take-home pay drops by only $2400.

At the risk of sounding like a late-night infomercial, we are not done yet. All of the money in your 401K grows without *any* tax consequences until you begin withdrawals at retirement. If you start contributing when you are young, you have a huge window of time before you can withdraw without penalty. As discussed earlier in this chapter, a long investment period can virtually eliminate risk because time can smooth out the short-term fluctuations.

So what would the long-term consequence be of giving up $2400 a year starting at age 25. Figure 7.1 assumes a 401K contribution of $4800 (as calculated above) per year with a growth rate of 10%. It shows that your 401K can grow to nearly $5,000,0000 by age 70. Remember, I'm not trying to tell you what's right for you. Maybe having millions when you retire is not worth $200 a month to you? But at least now you have one more option in your financial plan and know the consequences of acting on it.

The investment options inside most 401K programs include an assortment of mutual funds. As discussed in the last chapter, in order to reduce your risk and increase your return, you should select a diverse variety of funds. You should have exposure to large and small cap stocks as well as growth, income and value oriented funds.   You will also want some exposure to foreign stocks. The exact percentage of each type is not that important as long as any one type does not dominate. Since there are no tax consequences for buying and selling inside a 401K account, you can balance your funds whenever normal market fluctuations cause significant changes to your selected percentages.

Perhaps it has occurred to you that you might not work for the same company over your entire lifetime. When you change jobs its easy to transfer your 401K to your new employer or to move it to a self-directed IRA. The later is often the best choice because you can move the IRA to any mutual fund company. This allows you the flexibility of choosing a company with the fund choices you desire and the lowest expenses.

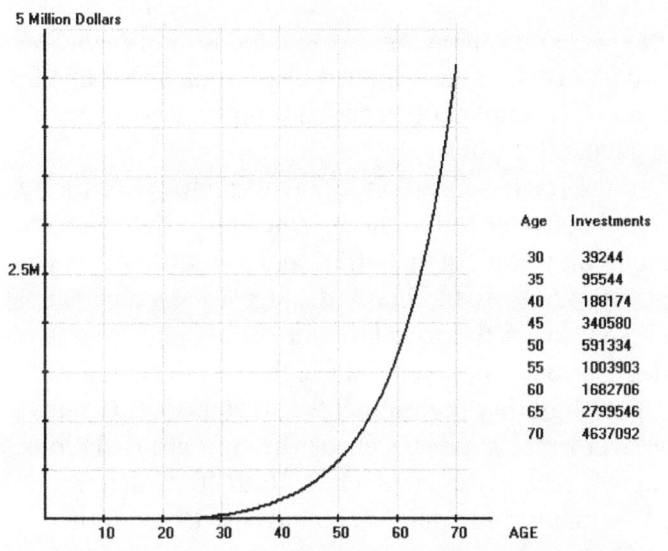

Figure 7.1: Even a modest 401K contribution can become millions by retirement.

A self-directed IRA has the same tax deferred benefits as a 401K. The fact that it is self-directed simply means that you can create or move the account to any mutual fund company or other financial institution that you choose.

Even if you participate in a 401K plan, you can open a self-directed IRA and contribute a few thousand dollars a year (the actual amount changes over time). If you are not participating in a 401K your contributions to an IRA are tax deductible just as they are in the 401K program. As great as a normal IRA is, a Roth IRA is even better. It is similar to a normal IRA but there are two major differences (and a few minor ones). The contributions to a Roth are not tax deductible, but you never pay *any* taxes on any of the earnings generated by a Roth.

Notice how this differs from a conventional IRA. In both cases there are no taxes as the IRA grows over the investment years. When you begin to withdraw from a normal IRA you must pay taxes on those withdrawals just as if they were normal income. With the Roth though, there are *no* taxes on the withdrawals. Think about this for a moment. The implications are enormous. Everyone should have a Roth IRA.

If you are really serious about investing for your future, you should consider fully funding (meaning contribute the maximum allowable) both a 401K and a Roth IRA. If you cannot afford to fully fund both, I suggest you contribute at least enough to a 401K to get the maximum matching funds provided by your employer and use the rest to fund the Roth. The eligibility requirements and contribution rates change over time, so always check the current regulations.

Congress recently created a new Roth 401K that is offered by many companies. You have to decide if the normal 401K (with its immediate tax savings) or a Roth 401K (where you pay taxes now, but never again) is right for you. If this book has convinced you that you should save and invest over your life, then you will probably find the Roth 401K better for you. Let's see why.

When IRA's and 401K's were created by congress, they assumed that people would have less income when they retired than when they were working. When that is true a standard tax-deferred account makes sense because you will be in a lower tax bracket when you retire than when you are working. If you invest properly though, your monthly earnings in retirement will probably be larger than your working income, in which case you would be better off paying taxes while you are working instead of when you retire.

If you are self-employed, you can create your own retirement system in the form of a SEP or Keogh. Both offer significant advantages over a normal IRA. Check with your business accountant for the current rules and regulations.

By now, it should be clear that you have many possibilities when it comes to investing for your future. In the next chapter, we will see how you can create a plan to ensure you will have the success you deserve.

Chapter 8
Creating a Plan

It is the purpose of this chapter to help you combine all the elements discussed so far into a plan. An appropriate plan should allow you enjoy the time you will spend working toward your goals, not just the goals themselves. Try to analyze your tastes and personality. Decide what things you really want from life and consider how much you might be willing to give up to get them.

The first step in accumulating wealth is to earn more money than you spend. You can do this by reducing your spending or increasing your income or both. You can increase your ability to earn by acquiring skills that are in demand or by increasing your education. When choosing the skills and education you want to acquire, you should consider in detail how they will be used. They could, for example, be used in a self-employment role or by working for a company that values your abilities. In both cases, you will be happier if you are doing something you value and enjoy.

The things your friends and relatives enjoy are not necessarily what's best for you. Going to work should be something you look forward to, not something you dread. Think about your hobbies and interests. Consider careers that allow you to participate in or contribute to the things you love. Whether your interests involve music or sports, problem solving or video games, there are opportunities that can challenge and excite you.

Once you have started a career as an employee or an entrepreneur you have the option of working overtime at your main endeavor or supplementing your efforts with moneymaking projects on the side. Remember, you have many options. You don't have to work long hours forever. As you have seen, once you build enough wealth, it continues to grow whether you contribute or not (Chapter 1).

Obviously, the wealth will grow faster if you can continue to invest by limiting your spending and avoiding debt (Chapters 1, 2, and 3). Again, it is important to realize that the sacrifices you decide to make don't have to last forever (Chapters 2 and 3). You can choose to save a moderate amount over your lifetime or you can choose to save nearly everything you make for only a year or two.

Understanding how and why the prices for stocks and bonds fluctuates (Chapter 4) is important. Not only can an understanding prevent worry, it can actually improve your returns because you will react more intelligently to market fluctuations.

As your wealth begins to grow, you need to prevent disasters so that all your hard work and sacrifice won't be negated. Maintaining appropriate insurance can handle the big unexpected disasters than can destroy your life (Chapter 5). Establishing a cash reserve can prevent normal periodic expenses from becoming emergencies. Improving your returns is important, but the risk of doing so must be evaluated and matched with your personality (Chapters 4 and 5).

You need to understand the various investment tools available to you (Chapter 5). These could include regular and Roth IRAs and 401K plans, and a wide variety of mutual funds and similar financial instruments. If you are self-employed, consider a SEP or Keogh plan.

When you structure your mutual fund investments create a mixture of various investment styles such as income, growth, and value. Make sure you are exposed to both foreign and domestic companies in all sizes (Chapter 5). When you invest outside of retirement accounts use index funds or tax-friendly managed funds that help you keep more of what you earn (Chapter 6). If you have at least five or ten years before you need portions of your portfolio consider taking more risk by investing in emerging growth or other high yield funds. An appropriate long-term plan, time can reduce or eliminate much of your risk (Chapter 5).

Unfortunately, many people plan to do all of the above, but fail in a few months. Others last a little longer, but end up failing just the same. Let's examine a few of the many reasons this happens. One of the major reasons people fail when they start to save is that they do not create a large enough reserve to handle emergencies. If you find yourself constantly tapping into your investments to handle emergencies you will soon realize you aren't really saving anything. You might even be loosing money if emergencies force you to sell your investments during down periods (Chapter 5).

As we have seen, people tend to be emotional about their investments, but you can avoid some of the pitfalls associated with emotion by periodically balancing your portfolio instead of chasing last year's winners (Chapter 5). A good understanding of why stock prices fluctuate in the short-run (Chapter 4) will also help you stick with your plan during the bad times so that you can participates in the recoveries that follow.

Let's examine Figure 8.1. It is a copy of Figure 3.1. Notice that the value of your investments increases faster and faster as time passes. At the beginning, the total dollars are increasing very slowly. During the ten-year period from age 30 to 40, for example, the total increases by less than $60,000. During the ten-year period from age

60 to age 70 though, the total increases by nearly a million dollars even though the amount that *you* contributed during the same periods is exactly the same. The reason, as we have discussed in previous chapters, is that the earnings each year are based, not only what you contribute, but on the accumulated compounded earnings. This simply means that the bigger your portfolio gets, the faster it grows.

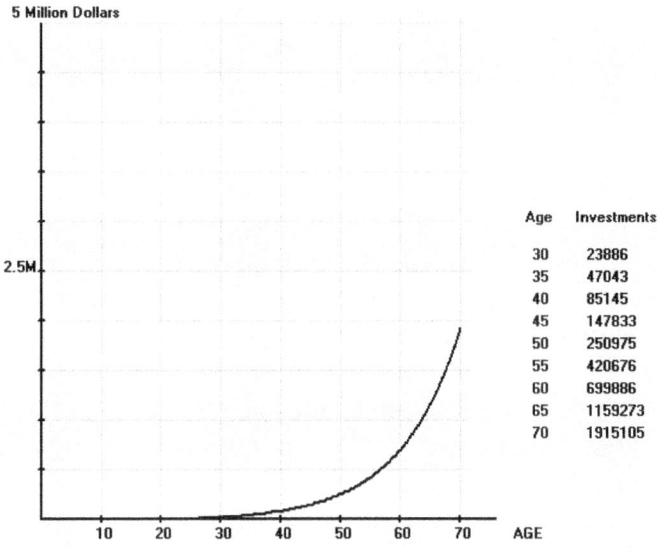

Age	Investments
30	23886
35	47043
40	85145
45	147833
50	250975
55	420676
60	699886
65	1159273
70	1915105

Figure 8.1: Investing only $100 a month can really mount up over time.

The fact that your total investment grows slowly at first and increases faster over time has several ramifications. It explains, in part, why many people stop their investing after only a short period of time. When they start to invest, the growth of their account is almost totally from their contributions. They do not see much in the way of progress and often quit because they become discouraged. If they can fight disappointment, and continue sacrificing and investing until the curve begins to climb, the feelings of disappointment often disappear.

There are two points on the graph that are very important. The first point is when the amount of money being contributed by investment returns is equal to the amount you are investing. In this example (where you are contributing $1200 a year) this point occurs when your total investment reaches $12,000. Using a 10% return, the amount being contributed by the portfolio itself will also be $1200, the same amount you are contributing. This means that your total is growing by $200 a month, double what it was in the beginning. Most people that stick it out to this point will continue with their saving plan because they start seeing real progress.

The second important point on the graph is when the amount of money being generated by the portfolio is equal to the amount you earn per year at your job. At that point you feel like you could retire because your investments are paying you as much as your job does. You should keep working though, for a several reasons. First, the income from your portfolio could fluctuate dramatically from year to year, so you might not have enough to live on during bad times. Second, inflation will slowly increase your cost of living. Historically, the amount of money you need to maintain the same standard of living will double every twenty years or so. This can be a huge problem if you have many retirement years ahead of you.

The last reason you should keep working when your portfolio is contributing as much as you earn at your occupation is because you have reached a point on the graph where your money is really starting to work for you. Since your savings are growing at a fantastic rate, your account will increase tremendously each year that you postpone retirement.

Obviously, if you have invested properly over the years and have reached a stage where the income generated by your investments is substantial, you have many choices available to you. You could lower your standard of living and quit work immediately or perhaps maintain your standard of living and work part-time. Or, as just suggested, you could wait a few more years and live a worry-free life because you have all the money you need. The choice can alter the rest of your life, so evaluate it carefully.

As we have seen, in order to make intelligent choices you must be able to predict the likely consequences of your options. In today's high-tech world, it only makes sense that we utilize technology to make it easier to predict the ramifications of our choices. Chapter 9 will show you how a computer program can help you evaluate the options you are considering.

Chapter 9
Consequences: The Software

This book has offered many options for improving your financial life. So many in fact, that you need a better way to explore the consequences of your potential choices. As mentioned earlier, the graphs in this book were created by a program that will run on any Window's based PC.

The program is totally free and may be downloaded from the following web page.

www.ConsequencesTheBook.com

No installation is necessary. Although you can store it anywhere on your hard drive, you might just want to save it to your DeskTop so that you can run it with a simple double-click.

When you first run the program you will see the screen in Figure 9.1. The start-up screen cautions you to read the user license, which you should do. Basically, it tells you that the program is free for everyone to use and that you can give it away but not sell it. It also cautions you that the author is not liable for choices you make based on the software. Although this book tries to provide an educational introduction to investing and financial planning, the decisions you ultimately make are yours and yours alone. Historical stock market returns can give us an idea of what to expect, but no one can predict the future. Use what you have learned here as the basis for perpetual learning. With a long life ahead, you should expect enormous changes. Chances are that congress will pass new laws that alter not only our tax structures, but even the nature of business itself. Even so, your chances of success should always be better if you compare the consequences of your options before you make your decisions.

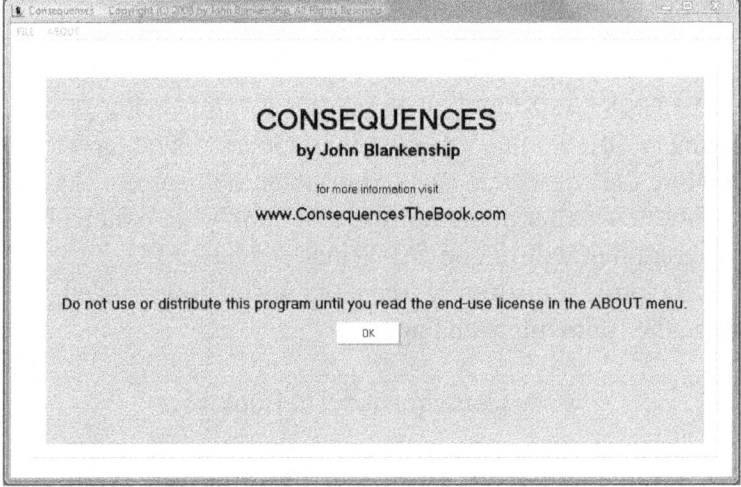

Figure 9.1: The start-up screen for
Consequences looks like this.

When you press the OK button in Figure 9.1, you will see the screen depicted in Figure 9.2.

Let's learn how to use the Consequences program by examining some of the claims made throughout this text. As you recall, Chapter 1 stated that you could amass nearly $70,000 if you saved only $6 per week.

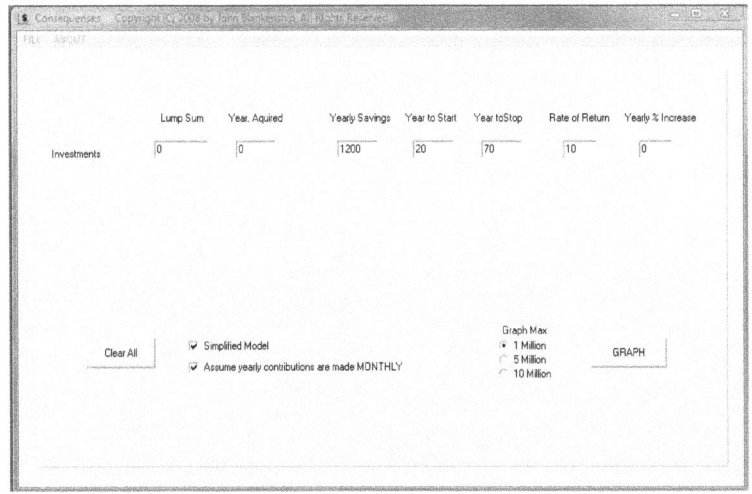

Figure 9.2: When you get this screen, you are
ready to explore your options.

Run the Consequences program and press OK to get the
screen shown in Figure 9.2. Click the **Clear All** button to
clear the sample data in the entry boxes. Click on the
Yearly Savings box and enter $72 ($6 x 12 months). Click
on the **Year To Start** box and enter 20. Click the **Year To
Stop** box and enter 70. Finally, click the **Rate of Return**
box and enter 10. You should see the data depicted in
Figure 9.3. (Note:You can save your data using the FILE
menu.)

Lump Sum	Year. Aquired	Yearly Savings	Year to Start	Year toStop	Rate of Return	Yearly % Increase
0	0	72	20	70	10	0

Figure 9.3: This data represents skipping
lunch once each month.

Press the **GRAPH** button and you will see Figure 9.4. It
displays a graph that shows how your investment will
grow. To the right of the graph is a column of numbers
showing how much money you will have at different ages.

83

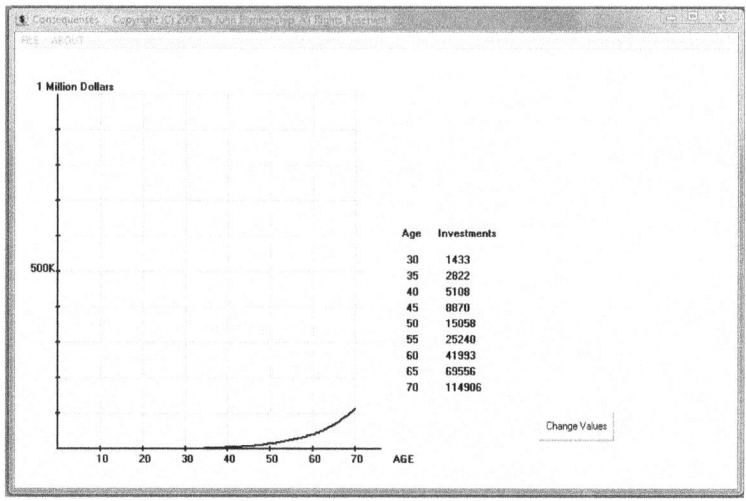

Figure 9.4: Just $6 a month produces
nearly $70,000 by age 65.

As you can see, the money grows to nearly $70,000 by age
65, but some new information is also shown. Waiting just
a few more years to age 70 brings the total to almost
$115,000. The power of compounding is awesome. Once
your sacrifices accumulate wealth, the wealth will work for
you. (Note: The FILE menu allows you to print the graph.)

Notice the **Change Value** button in Figure 9.4.
Pressing it will take you back to the data-entry screen so
that you can try various options.

Another option discussed in Chapter 1 was to give up
lunches for only five years. To evaluate this option enter
the data as shown in Figure 9.5.

Lump Sum	Year. Aquired	Yearly Savings	Year to Start	Year toStop	Rate of Return	Yearly % Increase
0	0	72	20	24	10	0

Figure 9.5: This data represents only
five years of sacrificing.

After entering the data, Figure 9.6 shows the results. If you
invest $6 each month ($72/year) from age 20 to 24 (5

84

years) and average a 10% return, you will have over $45,000 at age 70.

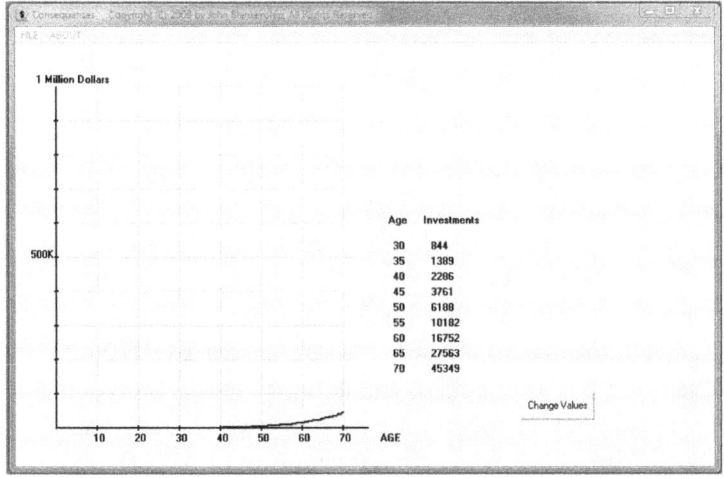

Figure 9.6: Just five years of sacrifice generates more than $27,000 by age 65.

Chapter 1 also pointed out that timing was very important. If instead of giving up lunches for the five years from age 20 to 24, what would the consequences be if you gave them up from age 61 to 65, the last five years before retirement? Alter the data and display the graph. Your accumulated total at age 65 will only be $464.

Imagine how helpful this tool can be. We know, for example, that investing $6 per month can result in nearly $70,000 by age 65 if you start at age 20. What would the consequences be for waiting until you were 22 or perhaps 25 to start? Consider examining other alternatives. For example, give up one lunch ($6) each week ($312/year) for a short time such as one or two years. Practice using the program by evaluating some of these or similar choices.

Once you feel comfortable with the program evaluate some larger sacrifices. For example, see how much you will have by retirement if you save $100 every month

($1200/year) starting at age 20. Enter the appropriate data using a 10% return and you will see that such a sacrifice will result in well over a million dollars by age 65 and nearly two million by age 70. Play around with these numbers. Evaluate how things will change if you wait a few years, or even 20 years, to start investing.

Try changing the percentage return on your investment to see how much the final number changes. Try increasing your return from 10 to 10.5 or 11. Try reducing it to 9 or 8. The enormous effect these changes have may surprise you.

The Consequences program has another option we need to discuss. Refer to Figure 9.2 and note the checkbox labeled **Assume contributions are made MONTHLY**. When this box is checked (the default option) the yearly contributions you specify are paid into your investment account monthly. A yearly contribution of $1200, for example, becomes a monthly event of $100.

If you uncheck this box, the program will assume you hold onto the money until the end of the year and then make a single payment to your account. Most people actually do it this way for standard IRA and Roth accounts. They might reconsider their behavior if they only knew the consequences of waiting until the end of the year to make their contribution. Using the data for the original $100/month example described earlier, uncheck the box and click **GRAPH** again. You will see that waiting till the end of each year to make contributions costs you about $65,000 at age 65. That is an enormous penalty for not taking the time to invest throughout the year.

The reason you don't make as much money if you wait till the end of the year should be obvious if you think about it. The money you contribute is simply not invested as long. Most people just never consider the consequences of waiting till the end of the year, and even if they did, it is doubtful they would predict such a huge effect. This example should impress you, especially when you realize that most people that plan to invest at the end of the year are putting the money aside monthly anyway. Generally, they just that they let it build up in a low interest checking or savings account instead of putting it to work right away.

Try several options to help you see how the program can help you evaluate a variety of alternatives. For example, try saving $1000 a month ($12,000/year) for just one or two years, starting at various ages. Also compare the results of any given plan if your return rates are either increased or decreased slightly.

There is another checkbox in Figure 9.2 labeled as the **Simplified Model**. This box is checked by default and creates the simplified data entry screen we have been using. Click the box to uncheck it and you will see the screen shown in Figure 9.7.

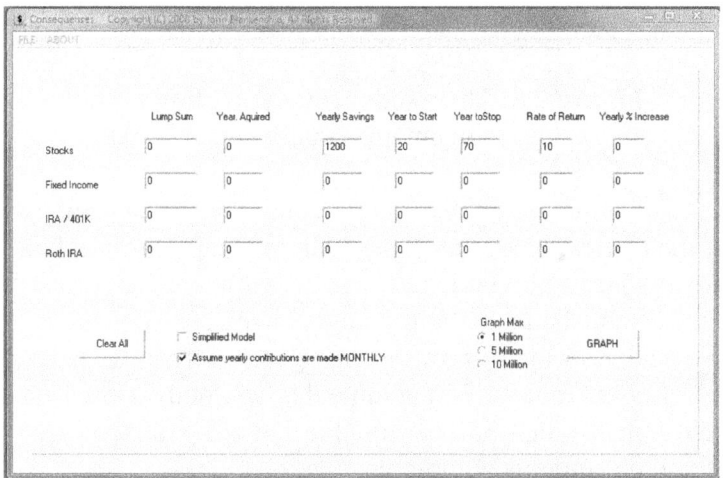

Figure 9.7: The unsimplified model gives you more options to consider.

In the unsimplifed model, you have four different accounts for investing your money. This allows you to set up many different options to evaluate. Let's look at an example to demonstrate how to use this new mode.

Let's assume your first priority is to save a few months salary to act as a safety net as discussed in Chapter 5. Let's further assume that the take-home pay for your family is $3000/month and that you feel you can save $400 every month if you really try. We will assume that you save the full $400/month for two years to create your safety net. In the years to come, you will use money from that account to pay for large unexpected expenses.

Since the money in this emergency account must be available at a moment's notice, we will assume it is in a saving account that only earns an average of 2.5%. Figure 9.8 shows how to enter this information.

	Lump Sum	Year. Aquired	Yearly Savings	Year to Start	Year toStop	Rate of Return	Yearly % Increase
Stocks	0	0	0	0	0	0	0
Fixed Income	0	0	4800	22	23	2.5	0
IRA / 401K	0	0	0	0	0	0	0
Roth IRA	0	0	0	0	0	0	0

Figure 9.8: The fixed income row shows how to maintain a safety net.

Let's examine Figure 9.8 to make sure you understand each of the entries. We are still assuming you are starting this process just out of college at age 22, which means you will have established your safety fund at age 23 (two years). We have no way to show the emergency withdraws from this account, but we will assume that you budget a reason-able sum (perhaps $50 per month) that will effectively repay the amounts withdrawn.

This means that, from age 24 on, you have $350 each month to contribute towards your investment goals. This number is calculated by subtracting the $50 you are going to budget for emergencies from the $400 you have available.

Lets assume you decide to invest $150 of your $350 in stocks using mutual funds. In general, you plan to use that money for retirement, but we will also assume that, if the market is doing well when you are about 35, you want to remove $10,000 from that account to use as a down payment on a house. Figure 9.9 shows how to make these entries into the program. Let's go over these to make sure they are clear.

The first two columns show that you are withdrawing (because it is negative) $10,000 at age 35. Of course, if the market is down then you might put off buying a house for a few years. On the other hand, if the market does really well for you, you might buy the house sooner.

The data entries show you are contributing $150/month ($1800/year) starting at age 24 until age 70. We are assuming you average a 10% return, but since this is not a retirement account you will have to pay taxes on your earnings. Therefore, we will reduce the expected after-tax returns to a reasonable 7.5%.

That leaves us with $200/month to invest. Let's assume we use half of that for a Roth account. Let's also assume that your company offers a 401K option for you and that their profit-sharing and other matching contributions, along with your tax break (see Chapter 7) allows your effective 401K contribution to be $200 even though your paycheck drops by only $100. Since we do not need to consider tax consequences for either of these accounts, the expected average returns will be 10%. Figure 9.10 shows the entries for both of these situations. After the above discussions, I will assume you understand each of the entries.

If you click the GRAPH button, you will see that the totals for your accounts far exceed the million dollar limits. Return to the data-entry screen and select **5 million** for the **Graph Max**. Click the **GRAPH** button again and you should see the screen depicted by Figure 9.11. There are five graphs shown, although one of them is so low on the screen it appears to be zero.

	Lump Sum	Year Aquired	Yearly Savings	Year to Start	Year toStop	Rate of Return	Yearly % Increase
Stocks	-10000	35	1800	24	70	7.5	0
Fixed Income	0	0	4800	22	23	2.5	0
IRA / 401K	0	0	2400	24	60	10	0
Roth IRA	0	0	1200	24	70	10	0

Figure 9.10: A complete plan utilizes many
different types of accounts.

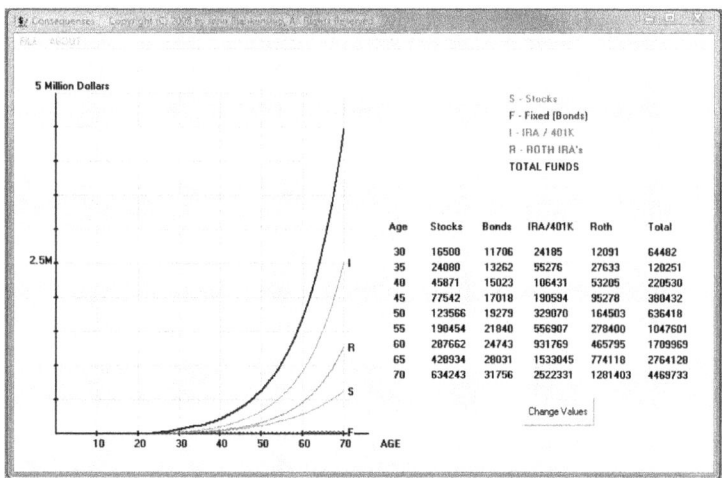

Figure 9.11: If you utilize the opportunities available, the
rewards can be great.

In order to make identification easier, each of the graph
lines is in a different color if you view this screen on your
computer. The lines are also labeled with **S** for stocks, **F**
for fixed-return investments like bonds, **I** for IRA or 401K
investments, and **R** for Roth investments. Notice also that
the amount in each account at various ages is shown in the
columns to the right of the graphs.

The fixed funds grow very slowly for two reasons.
First, we stopped adding money to the account after age 23,
and second, the returns on that account were assumed to be

very low. The stock account did much better, accumulating over $600,000 by age 70. The Roth IRA did even better even though you were contributing less money to it. The reason, of course, is that the investments in the Roth account were growing tax-free and we assumed a reasonable long-range return of 10%. The 401K account did the best of all, again for two reasons. First, like the Roth account, we were able to assume a full 10% return. Second, we assumed that company matching and profit-sharing boosted our effective contributions. The total is very impressive.

Recall, that we assumed your family had a take-home pay of $3000/month. It would be unrealistic to assume that you would not get raises over the years. Let's assume you get promotions or change jobs etcetera, and that your salary keeps pace with inflation. Let's further assume that a reasonable amount of inflations, perhaps 3%. Because of your expected wage increases, let's assume you increase your 401K and Roth contributions by 3% each year. We can tell the program to do that for us by placing the desired yearly increase in the final box of the appropriate row as shown in Figure 9.12.

	Lump Sum	Year. Aquired	Yearly Savings	Year to Start	Year toStop	Rate of Return	Yearly % Increase
Stocks	-10000	35	1800	24	70	7.5	0
Fixed Income	0	0	4800	22	23	2.5	0
IRA / 401K	0	0	2400	24	60	10	3
Roth IRA	0	0	1200	24	70	10	3

Figure 9.12: The last column of the data-entry screen specifies the yearly increase for contributions.

The program expects the boxes used for data-entry to contain numbers (no letters or symbols). Anything else will cause an error that the program will ask you to correct. Place a zero in any unused box.

If we graph the data we get Figure 9.13. Notice the total of your accounts now exceeds six million dollars, so you might want to return to the data-entry screen and change the Graph Max to ten million.

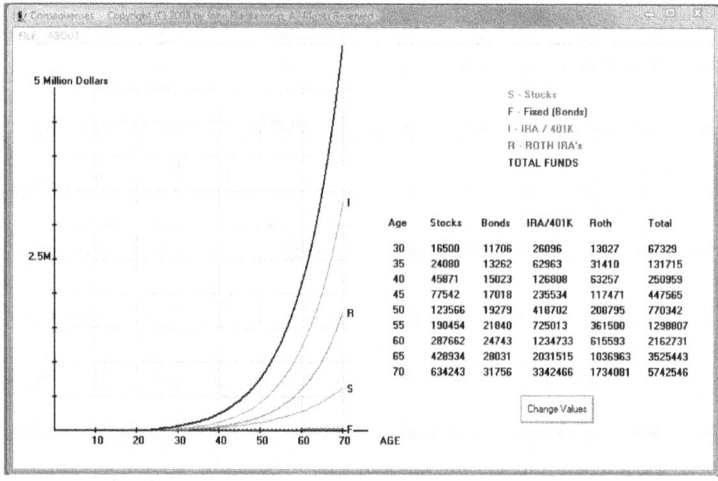

Figure 9.13: Increasing your contributions over time can ensure that your investments keep up with inflation.

Hopefully you can see how the Consequences program can assist you in evaluating options you might consider. Let's look at a couple more ideas to make sure the power of this program is clear.

Let's assume again that your family take-home pay at age 22 is $3000 per month but that you have convinced your parents to let you live at home for a couple years to help you get on your feet. Let's further assume that you are really dedicated to the ideas presented in this book and that you decide to give your parents a little to pay your share and keep a little to handle your necessary expenses, leaving you $2000 to save every month for two years. Use the simplified model and enter the data as shown in Figure 9.14.

	Lump Sum	Year. Aquired	Yearly Savings	Year to Start	Year toStop	Rate of Return	Yearly % Increase
Investments	0	0	24000	22	23	10	0

Figure 9.14: This data represents big sacrifices, but only for two years.

If you graph this data, you get Figure 9.15. As you can see, the end result is similar to the life-long investments described by Figure 9.12. Remember though, if you choose to make the big sacrifice for two years, you can spend *every penny you make* for the rest of your life and still retire with more than five million dollars – because the money you saved those first two years will continue to generate big returns for you.

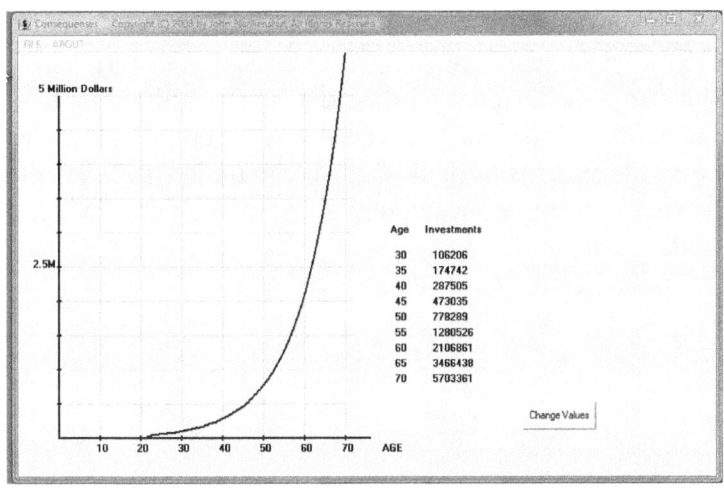

Figure 9.15: Big sacrifices for two years can pay off.

Neither of these choices might be right for you, but there are many in between. You might even consider part-time work for a short time, or perhaps marry someone with similar investment ideas.

Imagine how much money you could have if you and your spouse agreed to live on one income for five years, saving everything the other one makes. Better yet, put those numbers into the Consequences program and see what would happen. After five years, one of you could quit work to have kids and raise a family with no financial worries.

Perhaps you don't want to work until you are 65 or 70. Play with the Consequences program and find ways that allow you to have the money you will need to retire at age 50 or even 40 if that is your goal.

The important point is that *you have choices*. Explore your options, evaluate your choices, and then create a plan to make it happen. You can improve your life if you make appropriate decisions. We have seen the rewards of starting early, eliminating debt, reducing taxes, protecting yourself with insurance, maximizing your returns, and minimizing your risks. Decide which sacrifices are right for you by evaluating the consequences of your actions. And after you decide, you should have the will-power to stick with your decisions because you are confident in your future success. Confident because you understand *how* the sacrifices *you* have chosen will give you the things *you* want.

The choice really is yours.

Index